Lord,

WILL YOU DO IT?

A STORY OF A MOTHER'S JOURNEY TO HEAL HER
CHILD AND HERSELF

MARILYN KAY

First Print Edition: 2025

Published by: Open Arms Press

Written by: Marilyn Kay

Edited by: Karlee Renkoski

Cover Photos by: The Scarlett Lens

ISBN: Paperback: 979-8-9996476-1-0

ISBN: E-Book: 979-8-9996476-0-3

DEDICATION

For Emily and Julia,

You have been my sunshine, even before you were born. You've grown alongside me, and I've grown because of you.

We've experienced so much—laughter, tears, change, emptiness, victories, and all the in-between moments. Through it all, you've taught me more about love, patience, and what it means to show up.

I hope you continue to carry the love, strength, kindness, and curiosity I see in you.

No matter where life takes you, know that you are deeply loved not only by me but by God and that our story is my favorite one.

This book is for you.

For from Him and through Him and for Him are all things. To Him be glory forever.

(Romans 11:36)

INTRODUCTION

FOR ABOUT 25 YEARS, I thought this journey with my daughters, Emily and Julia, was so eclectic that I should write a book. Friends and family agreed. However, I knew I didn't have an ending yet.

In my late 40s, while daydreaming about my life, what it had become, and wondered what my future would look like, a thought came into my mind that I now know was the Holy Spirit. *I will have an ending to my book when I am around 60 years old*. At that time, this seemed forever into the future! But sure enough, in late 2023, I had an ending *and* a strong urge to sit down and write this book.

First, I created a vision board, where I added Ephesians 3:20: "Now unto Him that is able to do exceeding abundantly above all that we ask or think, according to the power that works in us." Then I began transferring my handwritten entries from 25 journals into a Microsoft Word document. They only covered a portion of the years I've spent with my daughters, so the rest of the book had to come from my memory. Often, these memories were hazy, but once I began writing, many of them came to life as though they happened yesterday.

As I sifted through my life stories, I knew I would need an editor to help me organize my thoughts eventually. And after months working on my book, this became more and more apparent. I have not been known to ask for help, in general, but I knew I needed it with a project as big and important as this!

One evening, I was giving a massage to a client who likes a quiet hour. As usual, my mind wandered, and this time it was asking God to present an editor to help me finish my book. The massage finished, and my client and I briefly visited. She told me they just hired a couple of really good people at her work who both have very nice wives. "One has a very unique business," she said.

My curiosity piqued, I asked her, "What is it?"

"She's a book editor! She helps writers become authors."

I was amazed. And excited! "Thank you God!" I exclaimed before explaining to my client, who was confused by my outburst, that I was in the process of writing a book. It was the quickest answered prayer I have ever received. He knew I desperately needed help too, which propelled me to continue!

Now, I was sure meeting this editor would be positive since I believed it was God answering my prayer, and it was! I immediately felt really good about her, and we began working together to craft this book.

I'll admit, writing about my life has not been a cakewalk. As I worked on each story, I encountered many emotions, including gratitude, love, sadness, frustration, hope, grief, anger, some regret, and laughter. I relived some traumatic parts of my life that were not fun to go through the first time and took the opportunity to heal from them, but I also felt joy when remembering the amazing events and people God placed in my path.

I had to view my life from a distance of sorts, all while profoundly feeling every decision, every event, every person so closely. And looking back, I can see that God was in it all, even more than I initially realized. So many times I felt completely alone, however, it was me who wasn't reaching out to Him for help and guidance.

It gives me so much joy knowing He was there all along and is with me now and forever.

When I had finished writing the draft of one of the most difficult chapters in this book, I had lifted my fingers from my laptop and sat back in my dining room chair with sadness in my heart. I closed my eyes and took a deep breath, feeling the warm sun streaming through my south window. Suddenly my Bible app sent me a notification. It was the Verse of the Day.

I opened it, and — oh my goodness — felt the Lord had given me a message so absolute and perfect to the moment that I couldn't ignore. I knew this was from Him and started giggling though there were tears in my eyes because I could feel Him with me. I thanked Him for giving me Isaiah 43:18-19: "But forget all that — it is nothing compared to what I am going to do. For I am about to do something new. See, I have already begun! Do you not see it? I will make a pathway through the wilderness. I will create rivers in the dry wasteland."

And I believe he has done just that!

My journey as a mother has been a roller coaster, but I am grateful for what God has taught me along the way and how He has directed my steps. And I'm excited to see how he will use my story to positively impact others.

This book was written with love, hope, and faith. A love for God. A hope for other mothers and families who have a disabled child and need a word of encouragement. And a faith that God loves us and has a purpose for every single one of our lives, no matter if we can see it right now or not.

This memoir is only a part of my story and that of my daughters', and I'm anticipating that God still has more incredible plans for us. The same is true for you too, and I hope that, while reading my book, you gain a sense of longing for the Lord and His purpose in your life.

MARILYN KAY

With that prayer over you, my readers, I will begin.

"For the Lord is good, His steadfast love endures forever." (Psalm 136:1)

PROLOGUE

ALL OF US HAVE memories that will never be forgotten. Many of these moments transformed us or called us to meaningful direction in our life. Some of them even seem out of the ordinary until we come to understand them years later. For me, one moment that I'll never forget occurred just before I graduated eighth grade.

I was attending St. Martin's Catholic school, and the girls in my class were invited to spend a weekend at one of the oldest buildings in St. Louis: the Motherhouse. It was to be a time of meditation, prayer, praise, and singing. Most importantly, it was a weekend that would reveal to us if there was a calling on our life to become a Catholic nun.

Although I thought I was too immature to consider this, Mom and Dad agreed that it was a good idea to go. As a family, we attended Mass every Sunday, and my great-grandfather even helped build the area's first St. Martin Catholic Church back in the early 1890s, so I think my parents viewed this as an opportunity for me to do not only some heart-searching but also better understand and appreciate our faith. Therefore, off I went with a few other girls from my school.

We were to stay at the Motherhouse itself as this would allow us to see how the nuns live on a regular basis. Upon arriving, we received our room designation and were told to get settled in. I was uncertain about what I would see when I opened the door to my room, and when I did, I'm pretty sure my mouth fell open and my heart undoubtedly sank. It looked like a prison of sorts, and my first thought was, *I don't want to stay here.*

It's not that I was used to a lot of comforts back home; my family wasn't rich by any means. But this room was even more minimalistic than I could have ever imagined. It was nearly empty, consisting of just a twin bed that squeaked, a wooden desk with a spiral notebook and pencil on top, a chair, a narrow closet, and a small window, which was a relief to see. The mattress was lumpy and bare.

I didn't know I was supposed to bring sheets and a blanket with me. My cheeks flushed with embarrassment when I had to ask for bedding from one of the nuns who came to my rescue. Overall, it was simply a bit depressing.

I was also shocked that, at my age, I was going to be living there over the weekend without a roommate. Although I was a very introverted person, my sister and I shared a bedroom at home, so the quiet environment of my room at the Motherhouse felt uncomfortable. However, once out of my room, the nuns and the other visiting girls were very welcoming.

We did many activities over the course of the weekend — the harmony singing was my favorite — but what I remember the most was the property's walking trail used for meditation, reflection, and prayer. Along this trail were a few white and weather worn concrete statues. But there was one that I can still picture in my mind to this day: The Blessed Virgin Mary. She was poised on a pedestal and wearing a shawl that cascaded over her hair and dress. Her arms were outstretched, palms open to the sky, and her head was tilted downward as if looking invitingly at those who passed by.

It was there where I stopped to pray.

I tried to meditate but had never been able to focus easily, so I turned to the familiar Hail Mary prayer and then flippantly threw in an Our Father for good measure. *What am I doing here?* I thought. *I'm only thirteen. How will I even know if I hear from God?*

But ...

In the midst of my unsettling thoughts, a wave of sadness fell upon me, and I started to quietly cry. *What is wrong with me?* I frantically peeked around the area to make sure no one was watching. Relief washed over me when I realized I was alone, but I was still confused. And embarrassed. *Why am I crying?*

A few large raindrops began to fall sporadically, even though the sky didn't appear to be cloudy. It almost seemed as if God was sending these sprinkles just for me.

I was still lost in my thoughts when my friend Lynn suddenly appeared on the path. She asked if I was okay. I replied that I was fine with a half giggle and wave of the hand as if nothing was wrong while wiping tears from my face. How was I to explain it to her when I didn't even understand it myself? I made an excuse to return to the main house to avoid getting wet. But really, I wanted to run away from these unfamiliar emotions. And yet, as I walked away, another part of me felt I should stay in this moment with Mary a little longer ...

That evening after dinner, a young nun led our small group in song. I noticed that there was a peaceful spirit about her, and although part of me wanted that quality, I knew it didn't come naturally to me. My mind continued to drift in and out with thoughts about the strangeness of the Motherhouse and the lifestyle of the nuns. As another stirring song began to play, a truth arose within me: *I want a family. Two or three girls to be exact.*

By the end of my weekend at the Motherhouse, there wasn't a doubt in my mind. I knew I would never be a nun.

Years later, I still haven't forgotten that overwhelming and confusing emotion I felt at Mary's feet that led to a subconscious and perhaps prophetic moment during worship. And, I've never regretted my choice, even as I look back at the journey God had planned for my life.

Trust in the Lord with all your heart, and lean not on your own understanding; in all your ways acknowledge Him, and He shall direct your paths. (Proverbs 3:5-6)

PART 1

CHAPTER 1

It was May in 1989, and I was walking — more like waddling — into a JCPenney regional awards dinner eight months pregnant. I can't say I was feeling very well, but it wasn't just due to the pregnancy. My husband and I had grabbed a cab from the airport to our hotel after landing in Chicago, and the driver had taken us on a bit of a wild ride. Do you remember the Cheech and Chong movie in which the taxi passengers are waving the American flag while being jostled from one side of the cab to the other, grinning? That was our initiation to Chicago, only I wasn't smiling.

The reality, though, was that I wasn't supposed to be flying on a plane while that far along in pregnancy, or riding in that turbulent taxi. However, my doctor had given me special permission to fly to this awards dinner, and I wasn't about to miss it because it was at this event that the JCPenney Regional Merchandiser winner would be announced ... and I was in the running.

I had started working on the sales floor at the JCPenney store in our local mall just after college. For some reason, applying for a managerial position seemed too big a step for me. I suppose I didn't feel qualified. But in no time, I was moved up to a Merchandise Manager Assistant position, and not too long after that, my boss pulled me aside.

"I didn't know you majored in textiles and clothing and have a business minor," he said with astonishment.

Then he told me I needed to interview for the Merchandise Manager trainee program. So I did, and I got the job after a very long certified interview.

This training was exciting and gave me confidence in my business skills and clothing industry knowledge to take on my first departments as a manager: accessories, lingerie, and cosmetics. After a couple of highly profitable years, I got bold and asked to be promoted to Senior Merchandise Manager. Getting a promotion this quickly was unheard of at the time, but my boss received approval from his district manager, and I was transferred to the Men's Department where I sought to increase the company's profit, and mine. I wanted to prove that they had made the right decision in promoting me.

While I was keeping my nose to the grindstone, thankfully, others would remind me to have fun on the job once in a while. I happened to work with my sister-in-law, Amy who was a joy to work with. We enjoyed helping each other merchandise our departments when the seasons changed.

There was also Mr. Rod Schweitzer, the Assistant General Manager, who was a positive boss and someone I always looked forward to learning from and working with. Not only did he respect me on a professional level, but over time, he became like a big brother to me. And like most brothers, he had a bit of a goofy, mischievous streak.

One day as I walked into his office, he turned his head away from me, his hand over his mouth, and let out a big sneeze. When he swiveled back around, he displayed a handful of fake green slime. We belly laughed until my stomach hurt and I finally had to leave the room, but as soon as I walked back to his office, the laughter broke out again. After the third time trying to talk seriously about whatever it was I had come to say (by this time I had forgotten), the giggles still hadn't subsided, so I gave up and went back to work.

Over time, all my efforts in the Men's Department at JCPenney paid off. Every February, JCPenney held a Merchandiser Contest of the Year. It began in-house, so each individual store had to choose its winner who would then go on to compete at the district level. At that time, biker shorts were a fad, and although my store was the smallest in the district, we sold A LOT of them thanks to Rod's intuition to buy more than anyone in our district. That trend, plus my department's success with sales and profit overall allowed me to not only be chosen within my own store but also to win District Merchandiser of the Year.

I was excited and in disbelief. You see, this was happening to *me*: someone who didn't have a great GPA in high school and achieved a low ACT score; someone who was told at my high school senior counseling appointment that I wasn't college material (that stung!); someone who, after going away to college anyway, actually struggled through many of my classes. Yet somehow I had achieved the biggest number of department sales and made the biggest profit for JCPenney in our district for that year's contest. I knew I had worked really hard, but there was still a small part of me that believed the lie that I wasn't smart enough. So, I was overwhelmed and elated at receiving recognition for all I had done.

But it didn't stop there. My information was submitted for the Regional Merchandiser of the Year award, and that's what brought me to Chicago despite being eight months pregnant.

As I sat at the table with my husband, my boss, Rod, and some of the others who had been selected from our 800-store region, I could barely listen to the speeches being made. I was excited, and also nervous. *There is no way it will be me*, I thought to myself. *There's got to be someone else in all these stores who beats my sales and profit. I work at the smallest store in my district.*

Yet when they finally announced that year's winner, I heard my name. MY

NAME!

Holy Crap! I was stunned. I looked at Rod in disbelief. Then my husband. Then, back at Rod again, who gestured for me to head to the podium. So there I went, up to the stage as quickly as a very pregnant woman is able, and delivered my short and sweet speech of surprise and thankfulness, giving my team of associates a lot of the credit.

The next day, after an uneventful cab ride (thank God) and flight home, I was back at work. About lunchtime, I found Rod deep in thought at his desk reviewing some paperwork. I knocked quietly on his door to see if he had time to visit.

"So," he said when he saw me, "What are your plans?"

"I'm going to Wendy's for lunch," I replied. "Why? Do you want me to bring something back for you?"

He laughed. "No, I mean, what do you want to do within the company? Once you win the regional award, you can declare what you want to do, and the company makes it happen. They'll transfer you wherever you want to go."

I took a seat across from him, my head spinning. *Wow! It's possible to receive a promotion because of a company award?* My heart started beating faster as I realized that this was the chance of a lifetime.

Since the day that I had signed up to go to college, my dream was to be a buyer for a major department store's home office. In my heart, I knew that's what I still wanted. I also knew that although JCPenney's current home office was located in New York City, a new one was being built in Plano, Texas. I wasn't sure how easy it would be to move while pregnant, but I definitely wasn't against calling Texas my new home.

My excitement grew ... until I realized I'd have to try to sell this career opportunity to my husband.

Despite my eagerness, when I shared it with him and the rest of my family, they didn't feel the same way about the job offer that I did. And they weren't supportive, possibly because I was about to be a new mother. Their response, added to my increased hormone levels from pregnancy, gave way to so many emotions. I was hurt, disappointed, and angry.

There were other thoughts, as well, but of course, I didn't want to leave my husband and raise our baby on my own. I couldn't imagine juggling a career and childcare in New York City or even Plano for that matter. But it was hard seeing my dream so close to my fingertips yet not being able to grasp it. Then I had to watch, as it slipped away.

Later, when the home office was moved to Texas, our store received a picture of the new facility, which hung on the wall in our administration office. So many times, I would walk past it and think, *I could have been there*. But God had other plans.

Although I didn't get to follow that dream, I will still forever be grateful that I achieved the coveted regional award that year at JCPenney. It was a pivotal moment for me, and not just for my career. Rather, it had solidified that I could succeed at this thing called "life," and this would be especially important in the months to come.

"Now faith is confidence in what we hope for and assurance about what we do not see." (Hebrews 11:1)

CHAPTER 2

My BEAUTIFUL EMILY WAS born right on time on June 12, 1989. I could tell she had my husband's hands, and I was completely taken with her adorable little nose and dark hair. Unfortunately, it was a difficult delivery and she was in the birth canal for a long time. Her head was cone-shaped, but the doctor told me not to worry and that it would shift back to normal.

When they laid her on my stomach, to be honest, it was such a strange feeling because she was still covered with that white cheesy stuff. Then they cleaned her, and I very quickly grew to love the snuggles and the way her breath tickled my neck as she lay on my chest all cozy. She had the sweetest smell that I will never forget.

Emily became the center of my husband's and my world, and I couldn't imagine life without her or how we ever thought life was good before she arrived. As we settled into parenthood, I found that the evenings were my favorite time. I loved rocking Emily while singing "You are My Sunshine" and reading her books, even though she couldn't understand them yet. I would watch her dad hold her up to the mirror and tell her how pretty she was and think about how blessed we were.

Even though I still loved managing the Men's Department, my work became secondary to motherhood. There were more days of exhaustion than not, but I loved my life with my baby girl and wished I could be with her all the time. Motherhood, I discovered, was sometimes overwhelming but also a remarkable gift and a privilege that I held very close to my heart. I loved being a mom, and it totally outweighed the moments of exhaustion.

I wanted to be the best mom ever, a great role model, and a cheerleader for every milestone she would experience. I cherished the countless and priceless moments, and I already held dreams in my heart for Emily that gave me so much joy. I never imagined I could feel so strongly about another human being and knew I wanted more children, but not yet.

However ...

Surprisingly, Julia was conceived six months later. The pregnancy was very normal until the evening of October 14, 1990. I had been extra tired at work that day, so much so that I couldn't put one foot in front of the other and my body would just drop into a chair when preparing to sit down. Upon arriving home, I felt a trickle that didn't stop and knew something was not right, so I called the doctor.

"It sounds like your water broke!" he said. "Why are you still at home?!" My heart sank. I was having my second child six weeks early.

My husband and I dropped Emily off at her Aunt Amy and Uncle Jerry's house. They were always there if I needed them. Then we headed to the hospital. It felt like the drive was in slow motion, and in my total exhaustion, all I could do during it was pray silently. Even though I knew the situation wasn't good, I still had strong hope that all would be okay and life would move on as expected, smoothly as before. I consoled myself with the thought that many other children were born early, some even at an earlier time of gestation, and they grew up normally. So, adamantly, I declared to myself that my child would be just fine too.

Julia was born the next morning at 7:12 a.m. She was so tiny. Her head fit in the palm of my hand. She was also very thin, had no hair, and her preemie clothes were too big. Yet she was amazing. Her Apgar score was 7 and 8, which meant she was healthy, though she still had to be watched in the NICU. I had a room elsewhere and was exhausted after being up all night, so I fell asleep and woke up throughout the day when my family arrived or when I wanted to check on Julia in the NICU.

The NICU was unsettling. There was only one other baby in the room with Julia that night, and it was under a Bili light in the corner screaming and banging its head against the crib. It was so sad, and I was alarmed when the night nurse did nothing. In fact, she was unresponsive with me, my family, and even the other nurses who came by to help. I stayed with Julia for a while and felt uneasy when I had to leave her at 8 p.m., but I needed more rest.

About an hour or so into sleep, I was awoken by the Level 1 nurse. "I have some bad news," she said. "Your baby coded."

"What do you mean?" I asked groggily.

"Your baby stopped breathing, but we were able to bring her back. She's stable now." She went on to tell me that Julia was still having some Apnea but asked if I would like to see her.

I sat there trying to process what she was saying, but I was numb. I didn't understand. *How could her Apgar score be good but then her body have this episode?" And if I go see her, what will she look like?* I didn't know if I wanted to be shown the reality of what had happened to Julia, but I nodded to the nurse anyway. *Please, God, let her be okay.*

Still shaky from giving birth and now a ball of frantic nerves, I wondered what I'd see. We made the short walk from my room to the NICU, my feet feeling like they were dragging behind me, and my fear was realized. Julia was on an oxygen hood, and there were wires and monitoring devices attached to her. I wanted to hold and hug her, or even just touch her, but I didn't know how or if I should. The nurse began explaining what was happening, then suddenly ...

Julia was coding again right in front of me!

As I stepped back so the medical staff could help her, I felt myself detach from my mind and body. It was as if I was observing everything as someone else or I was in a dream, yet what I saw was a nightmare unfolding. *This isn't really happening.* Julia's whole body turned black and blue. Her arms and legs were flailing out stiffly away from her body like she was feeling for something to cling on to. Time stood still as I watched her totter between life and death, hoping she'd cling to life.

She was gone for about 10-15 seconds, but it felt so much longer than that. Once they had bagged her and brought her back again, they also had to intubate her so she could continue to breathe. I was relieved she was pink again, but I really didn't know what losing oxygen meant for a baby. Except that it was not good.

The hospital staff decided to transport Julia to the University of Missouri Hospital, about 30 miles away, where she could be better cared for. They asked who they could call to be with me in the meantime. My sister, Kathy, arrived, and together, we watched Julia fly away in a helicopter through my hospital room window. It was a relief to know she was heading to a Level 3 PICU. My concern now turned to Emily. I had been away from her for too long, but Kathy assured me that Emily was safe at home with her dad and likely sleeping soundly.

The next morning, they released me, and I drove straight to Julia. To my relief, the hospital staff had taken very good care of her. She had been given a blood transfusion, and they said she was a happy camper after that.

"She just needed blood," they reassured me.

Julia spent two weeks in the PICU there, and before she was released, the neurologist came to see her. During his examination, he picked Julia up in a precarious way, holding her by the back of her neck like a puppy. I was stunned, which I'm sure he could tell by my facial expression, especially since she was a preemie, only 4 pounds and 3 ounces. I then watched as Julia's legs started moving stiffly as if she was walking or pedaling a bike.

When the doctor finished his assessment, he turned to give me the bad news. "Julia may have some trouble walking or she may not walk at all," he coldly explained. "She may not talk either due to the loss of oxygen she experienced. But only time will tell."

This news from the neurologist only made me more frustrated. I listened to his words quietly, but as we drove our little miracle baby home, internally, I was shouting in defiance.

My baby is going to walk and talk!!!

"But forget all that—it is nothing compared to what I am going to do. For I am about to do something new. See, I have already begun! Do you not see it? I will make a pathway through the wilderness. I will create rivers in the dry wasteland."

(Isaiah 43:18-19)

CHAPTER 3

THE DAY JULIA AND I came home, my husband picked Emily up from her aunt and uncle's so that she could meet her sister. She entered the house and began walking nervously around the family room where I was sitting. Several times she glanced over to see what I was holding but continued to avoid me.

"Emily," I said invitingly, "Come say hello to your baby sister."

Finally, Emily decided to acknowledge Julia. She ran up to us, briefly looked at her, and said "baby." Then smacked her on the head!

Oh boy. We had just interrupted Emily's perfect little life of being the only one on the main stage, and the stage light may have just dimmed upon her. Being just 15 months old, she had no way to understand what was happening, but of course, we told her to be nice to her baby sister and "absolutely no hitting."

It was a whole new world adding a second child to the family dynamics, and so soon after Emily was born. I was playing it by ear. Even though I read the book *What to Expect the First Year* by Heidi Murkoff, no number of books could have completely prepared me for everyday life's ups and downs with two kids under two.

Julia — our fragile little China doll — was sleeping normally, eating normally, and was a happy baby. She curled up at my neck just like Emily did and I sang "You Are My Sunshine" to her the same as I did to Emily. But we knew something wasn't right. Julia's legs were so stiff, I had to bring her knees to her chest to get them to move apart to change her diaper. My husband and I rarely talked about this and simply waited for a switch to flip and regular development in this area to occur. Oddly, her legs felt very normal while she was sleeping, and this gave me hope.

Hesitantly, I went back to work in January 1991. Julia was diagnosed with pneumonia shortly after and was in the hospital again. She came home after a couple of days and thankfully recovered fairly quickly. Perhaps Julia had a weak immune system, but I believed she had contracted pneumonia from being around the daycare provider who swore she didn't smoke in the house (yet I saw the smoke when I picked up the girls unannounced). So, I found another babysitter.

The next was no better. I dropped in unexpectedly one day and heard Julia screaming at the top of her lungs. As I rounded the corner to the room, I saw her face was a deep shade of red and there was green snot running from her nose. She had been left alone to nap in the corner of a playpen, which had a particle board base, and there was no padding on top of it. I couldn't believe it.

At this point, I wanted to stay at home with my girls. Although I was very successful at my job, that didn't matter anymore. I loved my career, but it was no comparison to how much I loved my babies! This emotional tug-of-war began affecting me deeply. I knew we needed the money, but every day it became harder and harder to drive to work.

Emily was 18 months old when I noticed that she had a couple of lumps on her lower abdomen while dressing her. We took her to the doctor, and he said she had some hernias. Her little ovaries were popping through her abdomen. A couple

13

days later, Emily went in for surgery. I watched the staff take her back in a little red wagon. It might have made *her* feel better, but it didn't help my nerves. The surgery went well, though, and Emily thrived afterward.

She was smarter than I ever thought an 18-month-old could be. We read books almost every evening, and she loved it! *Good Night Moon* was one of her favorites. By age 2, she was reciting the ABCs and numbers up to 20.

At Julia's 3-month doctor checkup, we discovered she was growing in weight and height as a preemie should. She weighed what she would have weighed if she had been born on her due date. The doctor said she was doing great, but he noted that her legs were stiff.

My baby is going to be fine! I told myself.

Her 6-month checkup went okay. She was gaining weight like she was supposed to. She could roll over but was not crawling yet, so she was behind in physical activity. The doctor said it was normal for children who are born early. "Let's see what happens at her 9-month checkup."

I wasn't worried. *Any day, she will start to crawl.*

Julia's 9-month checkup came around fast, and she was not crawling yet, or sitting up. But she was showing signs of moving in an army crawl and would use one knee to help propel her forward. Her lazy eyes from the O2 given to her while a preemie hadn't converged together, so she would still use one at a time to see.

I noticed the concern on the doctor's face, but he said we would "see what happens at her 1-year checkup." I never asked any further questions. Maybe I was hopeful. Or maybe I was too afraid to hear any answers. By this time, the family was asking me about her development too, and I would give them a brief response. I didn't want to talk about it.

At Julia's 1-year checkup, the doctor referred me to another doctor at the University Hospital and Clinics in Columbia, Missouri, for testing. She was only army crawling and rolling over. She was not sitting up by herself at all but would lean to her right while in a chair to eat with her left hand. Because of this, her right hand was rarely used at mealtimes. Yet she was the happiest child, and with her temperament, you wouldn't even think she could have any issues with that huge smile and shining crystal blue eyes.

Our appointment at the clinic was in November of 1991. The doctor and her assistant performed all sorts of tests to assess Julia's progress and prognosis, and a month later, we came back to get the news.

"I'm sorry to tell you that your daughter has a slight case of cerebral palsy."

"The Lord is my shepherd, I shall not want; he makes me lie down in green pastures. He leads me beside still waters; he restores my soul. He leads me in paths of righteousness for his name's sake. Even though I walk through the valley of the shadow of death, I fear no evil; for you are with me; your rod and our staff, they comfort me. You prepare a table before me in the presence of my enemies; you anoint my head with oil, my cup overflows. Surely goodness and mercy shall follow me all the days of my life; and I shall dwell in the house of the Lord for ever."

(Psalms 23:1-6)

CHAPTER 4

I STARED AT THE doctor, speechless, for what felt like a full minute. *I don't know anything about cerebral palsy.* Finally, I asked. "What is that? And how do we fix it?"

She began by explaining that Julia has cerebral palsy on the spastic diplegia side. As she talked, I tried to listen, but all I could think about was that I was going to do whatever I could to make things right for Julia, to give her the best life possible.

My "get it done" attitude had just started building inside of me when I heard the doctor say, "Unfortunately, there's no cure."

What?! I was stunned, now fearing for Julia's future. *How can they say the word "slight" when telling us this? Julia's condition is not what I consider to be slight!! And, God, how could you do this to an innocent child? How could you do this to my family? No one else I know has children with a diagnosis like this!*

"Can there be improvements?" My voice cracked as I asked the question.

The doctor said there was a surgery that may help relax Julia's legs and feet and that we could get her into early intervention physical therapy too, which might help. She handed me the results and recommendations documents from Julia's testing to read over. In short:

NEUROLOGIC EXAM: Right esotropia. There also appears to be occasional fleeting inward deviation of the left eye. There is no evidence of cranial nerve deficits. Primitive reflexes are not present. Superficial abdominal reflexes cannot be elicited. Increased muscle tone is present in the trunk and extremities. This is relatively mild in the upper extremities and more severe in the lower extremities where there is frequent scissoring. The heel cords are tight and dorsiflexion at the ankle joint is not possible past 90 degrees. There are minimal contractures at the knee joints, which lack several degrees of complete extension. Deep tendon reflexes are exaggerated, particularly in the lower extremities. Plantar reflexes are equivocal. When prone, the infant raises her chest off the table and brings her knees under her, also raising her abdomen from the table. The thoracic and lumbar spine is posteriorly bowed with loss of the normal lumbar lordosis. The infant cannot sit unsupported horizontally above the table in a prone position, she holds her body rather straight in a horizontal plane with the face lying down. When lowered toward the table, she extends both arms symmetrically. She has no head lag when pulled to a sitting position. The shaking movements of the head and left upper extremity described by the mother are observed and appear to be voluntary.

The Denver II Developmental Screening Examination: in the personal social area, there is one caution; in the fine motor adaptive area, there is one delay; in the language area, no cautions or delays; in the gross motor area, four delays and one caution; Julia easily hears a bell rung softly several feet behind her and lateralizes the sound correctly to either side.

SUMMARY: According to Bailey's results, child performs at an 11-month age level in the mental area and 8 months in the physical area. This demonstrated a delay of 3 months mental and 6 months motor compared to the corrected age.

IMPRESSION: Spastic diplegia with no evidence at this time of cognitive or language delays. This is an appealing child with many obvious strengths. I feel that in this caring family, she will do very well.

RECOMMENDATIONS:

- Continue PT 3x weekly.

- Start OT 1-2x weekly to work on the following: normalizing tone, improving trunk control, and improving developmental skills including fine motor, eye-hand coordination skills, and assessment of oral skills.

- Position equipment to provide trunk support to have hands free for eating and developmental play activities. Recommend this take place as soon as possible to allow Julia the needed trunk support. This can be done locally or through our rusk wheelchair clinics at UMCH.

- Contact the regional center and inquire about the First Steps program.

- Start Parents as Teachers Program.

- Return to the clinic in 8 weeks. Plan to transfer follow-up for these services eventually to the Special Needs Clinic.

- Continue to treat Julia behaviorally as a normal child.

After I skimmed the test results, my mind saying "this can't be happening" over and over again, Julia's challenges seemed amplified. Although there were some positive parts in the document, my shoulders slumped even further, and my heart broke into tiny pieces.

Later that evening, during a quiet moment while sitting in my rocker recliner, the tears finally flowed. However, it wasn't too long before the slow back-and-forth movement of my chair quickened into a more purposeful pace. My sadness turned into determination. *Julia will get better! I will prove them wrong!* I wiped my eyes and made a note to myself to finalize appointments the next day for Julia to attend physical therapy at the local hospital.

And, in the midst of all the news about Julia's health and her special needs, one side of my constant emotional conflict quickly won out: I knew I couldn't continue working full time. Something had to change. My husband and I discussed the possibility of giving up my career. He said that if I could show that we would survive on one income, I could quit.

We could, barely.

So, I gave my leave notice to my manager but requested to stay on as a jewelry salesperson. I knew I could make the most money working part-time on commission. The change was accepted.

Two weeks later, I approached the General Manager's office to hand over my store keys. My eyes were misty, but I felt my smile grow bigger and bigger and a kind of heaviness lift off my shoulders. My manager at the time noticed my facial expression.

"Well don't look so happy about this!" he joked, but there was a hint of sarcasm in his voice too. He didn't want me to leave.

"Well, I am happy." I shrugged playfully then added more solemnly, "But, I will miss working with you and all the other managers."

This was the honest truth. I also knew I would miss the job itself. It had been my dream, and it was going to be hard seeing someone else planning, buying, and merchandising the floor during the next season.

However, walking away from my career was the easiest decision that I had ever made, and it was the right one. Now I could take better care of my girls and give Emily the time she deserved and get Julia the therapy she needed to beat this diagnosis.

"The Lord is near to the broken hearted, and saves the crushed in spirit."

(Psalm 34:18)

"The LORD shall fight for you, and you shall hold your peace."

(Exodus 14:14)

Chapter 5

Julia began physical therapy twice a week at the local hospital. The therapist was tough on her, which was hard for me to watch, but really good. However, by the end of that year, I had become disheartened by what Julia was receiving, and my husband and I believed some of her muscles were getting worse. Her feet, for example, were more spastic, and it seemed they could extend past zero degrees of her shins, which was not natural.

By this time, some family members were repeatedly asking us to see an orthopedic doctor to have Julia try surgery on her hamstrings, adductors, and heel cords. They loved Julia and only wanted the best for her, but I immediately didn't feel good about it. I called Shriners Children's Hospital St. Louis anyway, and they recommended all three surgeries to both legs at once and gave me information about what results other children had experienced and what to expect after surgery.

NO, I thought. *That is too intrusive. Three surgeries may need to be done, but I'm not putting Julia through all that at once.* Really, I didn't want her to have any surgeries, but to appease my family, I decided to try at least one with a well-known doctor.

Julia received the adductor tenotomy surgery — only to help her legs relax — and an eye surgery, which the doctor had wanted to do as early as possible, the same day so she wouldn't have to undergo anesthesia more than once. The surgery was followed by weekly physical therapy visits, but even after those, Julia's legs returned to where they started. Her body DIDN'T move any better than before! (The eye surgery didn't help her lazy eye either.) Not only that, but she had scar tissue now too.

I couldn't believe the healing process she went through after the surgery. The wound dressing caused her pain, and seeing her wrapped up like a little mermaid to keep her legs from moving too much was difficult, especially knowing what it looked like underneath. and then seeing her smiling her huge smile with those blue eyes dancing with joy living her little toddler life the best she could was a miracle to me. She didn't know it at the time but she helped me get through such difficult moments.

Her resilience astounded me.

I hoped someone else had benefited from this surgery, but my husband and I decided that continuing with the other two was out of the question, even after prompts from my family and others. Julia could choose to do it after she turned 18, but I wasn't going to let them cut her up like that ever again while it was my choice.

So, we turned to alternative treatments, which wasn't a popular medical avenue at the time. But since the best doctor in the field (supposedly) couldn't help Julia, why not?

First Alternative Treatment: Hippotherapy

The developmental doctor had informed me that there was horseback riding therapy for children with cerebral palsy. The closest one was located just 25 minutes from our home, so at about 3 years old, Julia started riding once a week in addition to her physical therapy.

It certainly relaxed her hip muscles, but it did little for her legs and extended feet. After about two summers of this, the trainers and I decided she was too small to benefit from hippotherapy. We quit going for the time being.

However, there was at least one major benefit from trying this treatment: We met another family that was in the same situation as us. Denise's daughter, Brittany, had been diagnosed with cerebral palsy. She was about a year older than Julia, and we discovered that they both were attending the same physical therapy hospital.

We ran into Denise and Brittany while we were heading to a physical therapy appointment and they were leaving one. Denise mentioned they were going to Mississippi to try a new therapy called Chronologically Controlled Developmental Therapy (or CCDT) at Futures Unlimited, Inc. She briefly shared what she knew about it, and I asked her to let me know how it went, hoping she would call me while in Mississippi to give me an update.

My whole self was in an anticipatory and excited mood. Something was telling me that Julia should try this treatment before I even heard back from Denise. I couldn't wait, so I used the number she had given me and made the call.

Ed, physical therapist and the company owner, answered the phone. We introduced ourselves, and I shared Julia's journey with him. In turn, he explained his treatment protocols at Futures Unlimited. He said something like this:

"Our program offers 5-7 hours of passive neuromuscular reeducation, sensory integration, hydrotherapy, and other aspects of natural physical rehabilitative methods. Treatment sessions include 14 days of neurosensory stimulation but can also be tailored to fit busy schedules. There are no days off, so we give treatment during the weekends as well. It is a unique environment, and clients find the

program to be relaxing. There are dimly lit rooms with blue, green, and red lights for different therapeutic reasons. Also, the rooms are very warm and humid, and talking is kept to a minimum for peacefulness and to keep the cortex quiet. Most gains the clients achieve remain after going home, so it is a brain reawakening, not just a one-time event.

Although it seems like one would have to work very hard to relearn and exercise the parts of the brain or nervous system that were damaged in an accident or trauma, we know that this is not the case. They may not be able to function normally, but they remember how to walk, run, reach out, and do other complex movements. It is then necessary to go back to the point of the developmental function that is available, apply passive stimulus that relates to that portion of the development, and allow the individual to progress at a natural pace. This is truly much faster than trying to teach around a disability, and the result is an automatic — not a relearned — response.

Think of it this way: When a computer freezes, just turning it off and/or plugging it back in to reboot it works, so that all the files come back as they were before the incident. This is much like what this treatment does for clients. Although a child with cerebral palsy loses many of these basic functions at birth before they have gone through all the normal developmental stages of crawling or walking, they can still recover some development and function regardless. Basically, our genetics contain all of the information needed for the recovery of lost function.

I would ask you to just try it. Better yet, come and let your daughter try it so SHE can show you what this treatment can do for her."

In my mind, I was already driving her to that clinic!

Sure, the treatment protocol did sound a bit crazy. Well, *very* crazy. But I did my due diligence and called the Mississippi Attorney General. There were no litigations. I called the Better Business Bureau to see if there were any past or current issues, and there were none. I called a couple more referrals, and everyone who I contacted and had experienced this treatment gave me great encouragement about it. Their loved ones had all received changes much quicker than traditional treatment or even after they had given up on traditional treatments. All there was left to do was wait for Denise to call with an update ...

When she did, it was only good news! Denise told me the therapy was very different, but after Brittany's third day, she was already showing signs of improvement beyond what she ever thought could happen.

My hopefulness grew, by leaps and bounds!

After a year of traditional physical therapy and Julia's feet tighter and more pointed than when she had started, I was ready to try CCDT. More importantly, I couldn't find a reason not to. My family was hesitant, and a couple of friends thought I was crazy, but I didn't care. I called Futures Unlimited and reserved a 2-week session, scheduling Julia's first intensive treatment.

"Be joyful in hope, patient in affliction, faithful in prayer." (Romans 12:12)

"O Lord, be gracious to us; we wait for you. Be our arm every morning, and our salvation in the time of trouble." (Isaiah 33:2)

CHAPTER 6

OUR FIRST TRIP TO Futures Unlimited was *very* long. Julia was just over 2 years old, and we were traveling with another family: Ron, Jennifer, and their daughter, Amber, who had also been diagnosed with cerebral palsy. I knew Jennifer from grade school, and she'd had Amber just nine months after Julia was born.

We hit the road at 6 p.m. to drive through the night, passing by St. Louis and Memphis on our way to Tupelo, Mississippi. At that time, we had no cell phones, just a MapQuest search printed for directions, so we missed an exit in Memphis (and not in a good part of town) but eventually made it to the clinic safely at about 6 a.m. I was exhausted; thankfully, Julia had been an easy traveler and slept most of the way.

We parked and got out to stretch our legs. Mississippi smelled different. Pine needles covered the ground, there was a hint of ocean air, and it was very humid, even in February. We entered through the open back door of the clinic, an old metal building that we later found out had previously been used as a daycare. It was dark, and on our way to the office, we walked slowly through a hallway.

As our eyes adjusted, we saw a line of small cubicles. Each one had a large and flimsy tractor tire tube hanging from the ceiling. As we rounded the corner, we found several other partitioned rooms with the following: a shallow pool, a hot tub-like tank with hanging greenery, more tire tubes with bean bags below them, and some massage tables.

"What are we getting into here?" Jennifer whispered.

I was trying not to judge anything, still clinging to what the referrals had told me.

Eventually, we found the door to the waiting room and office area. We checked in and were given the keys to our trailers out back. There was the option of a hotel room, but when the staff informed me that they had trailers we could reserve at a lower cost ($300 for two weeks), I jumped at the opportunity. My husband and I needed to be thrifty because we weren't sure yet if our insurance would cover this type of therapy.

After we settled into our new home for the next two weeks, Julia and I met Ed for an entrance assessment before one of the aides took her back to begin treatment. I was reassured by all of the aides that they do this every day, so I shouldn't worry about leaving her, but Julia started crying when I handed her over. Still, I chose to put my trust in Ed's previous speech and walked out the door. However, I couldn't help but wait outside to hear how long Julia would cry. She stopped within a few minutes, and I was relieved.

And so Julia began her new morning routine.

Second Alternative Treatment: CCDT

The first treatment recreated neurologically the "pre-reptilian time period." It was done in the pool room where only a faint blue light was emitted. The room was so dim that it took your eyes about a minute to adjust upon entering and consisted of a very warm and humid environment of around 78-80 degrees. They placed a harness around Julia's head and trunk to support her while she floated on top of the water, which was set at about 101 degrees. There was 30% oxygen blowing over the pool.

While Julia floated in the water, the aide gently moved her own hand in specific directions along each side of Julia's body like an eel swimming in the water. She also moved the water at the crown of Julia's head and bottom of her feet. Julia experienced this sequence for approximately 35 minutes.

Her next movement treatment was on an oil-slick therapy table that was covered with plastic. The slipperiness allowed Julia's body, even her legs, to move in ways it couldn't if the table were dry. Her hip joints seemed automatically looser with the rotation exercises, and she received specific shoulder movements too.

During this time, the aide also administered deep pressure at specific areas along each side of her spine, thighs, feet, arms and hands. She would gently press until she could feel the bone and then move to the next spot. This was done in dim blue, green, or white light depending on what was ordered by Ed.

The final morning treatment used one of the big black tires Jennifer and I had seen while walking into the clinic. The tire was hanging from the ceiling on a large hook, and Julia was curled up in a fetal position inside while in dim red light. As she rested, she listened to a heartbeat tape. All of this was used to neurologically imitate the womb.

Like me, Julia's favorite time of the day was lunch. We were told to keep the environment quiet and only visit or talk when necessary to keep cortical stimulation to a minimum. At 2 years old, though, Julia found it very difficult to do this. I couldn't say I blamed her either! The lunch creeped along somewhat silently, as even we parents found the silence nearly impossible.

After lunchtime, Julia cried again when I handed her off to the aides, but she settled down on their way to the tank room. This area was also very humid and warm and consisted of three hot tub-like tanks. Each tank was filled with water that was set at about 101 degrees. There were ferns and greenery hanging from the ceiling, and the room was in dim green light.

Julia was placed in another harness that supported her at the head and trunk, and the aides proceeded with the movement protocol for the "reptilian time period." The water treatment was Julia's least favorite. She didn't like when her ears went under.

From there, she again received movements and deep pressures on the oil-slick table. Lastly, Julia went back into the tire tube in dim red light and listened to the heartbeat sound.

When I finally picked her up and heard from her aides that she had done well, I exhaled. Julia's first day of treatment was over, and I could not wait to see what kinds of physical changes the next thirteen days had in store for her.

"I consider that the sufferings of this present time are not worth comparing with the glory that is to be revealed to us." (Romans 8:18)

CHAPTER 7

JULIA WAS SCHEDULED FOR an exit assessment with Ed on the fourteenth and final day of our visit to the clinic. I was so hopeful for improvements similar to the ones others I had spoken to had achieved, and I was not disappointed. In just two weeks, Julia had made more progress than in her one year in traditional physical therapy!

For example, Julia was now able to W-sit comfortably. It had been extremely difficult to get her legs in that position before. She was able to pull a See 'n Say toy toward herself with both arms. She even moved the lever on the right of the toy with her right arm — yes, her right arm! — while holding her balance the whole time. Since Julia's body was spastic, she usually leaned to her right, bracing herself with her right arm, which meant her left arm was used functionally and her right was not. Now, I was so hopeful she might be able to use her right arm and hand functionally after all! Some might consider these actions to be inconsequential, but for Julia, all of them were miracles.

As we returned home, my heart was full. Ed had given me a therapy program to do with Julia between visits to the clinic to keep up her progress. He said it was important to keep her cortex input, or cortical stimulation, to a minimum. This would allow the brain to not only heal but also feel, instead of think.

I improvised with a card table in order to give her the deep pressure massages and placed her on a bean bag where she could lie in the fetal position since she was so small. I even found a heartbeat tape to play on our cassette player. Since I wanted to do the best I could for her, I also called Ed with (what now seem to be silly) questions.

1. If she is crying in the tube, will it still work? *Yes*

2. Is stopping in between steps at the end of the day okay? *Yes*

3. How long should I keep her in the fetal position? *10 minutes*

4.) Is music or singing okay while in the tube? *Yes*

5.) Does it hurt if I forget to change the lighting during stroking? I forgot to do that from blue to green. *Try to keep the program light recommended on.*

6. I can't keep her in the fetal position, so I wrap her arms around her knees. Is that okay? *Yes, that's fine.*

7. Do I need anatomy pictures to do all the muscle strokes? *No*

8. Is it okay if some days it seems I am only getting half of the therapy done? *That's okay. Just do your best.*

9. Is it necessary to use oil every time for stroking? *Yes*

10. Julia tends to lean toward high-interest activities. Is this okay? *Yes, it can be normal. It's good that she's curious!*

All my questions were answered, and Ed was incredibly accommodating with his time. I could tell he wanted to help me help her.

The teachers at Julia's preschool, the Special Learning Center, which she started attending just after healing from her adductor surgery, were also very supportive of her new therapy and wanted to help. Over time, they even set up a room in the school with black plastic over the windows so that someone could administer her treatments while she was there. Some days, I would do half of Julia's therapy, and the staff would do the other half. This was a relief, especially after I discovered Julia enjoyed her therapy at school much more than at home.

... Or so I thought. Apparently, the staff called her their "runaway student" because she also often tried to crawl down the hallway to the front door to "go home."

Amber and Brittany attended the Special Learning Center too, so they were also able to get some of their therapy done during the day. Soon other children were wanting the same treatment, and when it was given (with the parents' approval), Tami, one of Julia's favorite teachers, told me that they were seeing benefits with them as well. For example, when deep pressure was given to the ADD or ADHD children, they calmed down and would ask for it to be done again later.

I was so pleased that the knowledge we had received was helping other children and their families. It was also extra confirmation that the therapy was actually beneficial. Changes were finally happening in our little part of the world, especially for Julia.

At this time, she was becoming more talkative — up to seven full sentences a day — and showing signs of having a gift for gab. She was more curious and had begun trying to open all the cabinets around the house. One day Julia had three half-dollar coins on the floor. She said, "Mom, look! Three!" I didn't think she knew any numbers yet.

Her hands had more dexterity, and her back seemed to be getting stronger and straighter. When she was on all fours and reached for something with one hand, her back was now curving like a cow instead of a cat. She had been attempting to raise her butt while W-sitting, and I only had to reposition her three times in her high chair instead of 15-20 times while she was eating. When we ate while sitting on the floor, she would clasp the snack with both hands, not using either to balance.

Even though we had not been talking about it, Julia began saying she wanted to "walk all by herself," and I wondered if it was possible with how much her leg movement had progressed. When I would carry her on my hip, Julia started to bring her legs up higher around me. Before, she could only extend them down and straight, which made it very difficult to hold onto her. While playing, she liked to rise to a tall kneel position. It wasn't very tall, and she fell a lot, but she would beg us to watch her when she tried it.

For parents with a disabled child, any small change is a big change that builds to an even larger ability and function for their child. I clung to small developments and would journal about as many of them as I could to confirm I wasn't seeing things when Julia presented another improvement. I had been told so many times that cerebral palsy kids just don't get any better.

But Julia was!

And to prove it, that March I took her back to the orthopedic doctor who had performed Julia's adductor surgery. I didn't tell him that we had been trying an alternative treatment; I wanted to get his true, unbiased opinion. He quickly noticed her trunk control was MUCH better than it had been and said she was ready for another surgery or to try Botox shots to relax her legs. This was all the confirmation I needed. CCDT was still the right choice for Julia.

We returned to Futures Unlimited the next April. During this visit to the clinic, I made sure to write down what I noticed in my journal:

April 12 - Julia was a "wired" girl at lunch today; very excited and happy. She did not cry much and ate well. I said, "Go tell Lindsey to come back with us." Julia said,

"I'm too busy." Her personality and character are different, and she is beginning to show it.

April 13 - Julia slept well but cried when I left. She is doing great in therapy. She is holding her cup up with both hands longer without dropping it or starting to lean to her right side. She is very happy ... talk, talk, talk!! Julia is beginning to ask "why" all the time. She held a big toy over her head with both arms for a short while. New!

April 14 - Julia plays with getting up on her knees quite a lot. Sang Happy Birthday To You today at lunch. Starting to wash not only the palms and hands together but also the forearms.

April 15 - Hands are being used more, and they are even more open than before. At TCBY she sat on a big chair holding on to the table and was comfortable; her legs didn't get tight. I was even able to leave her and get napkins without her being scared she would fall. She ate three-fourths of her Taco Supreme and fell asleep on the way home at 5:45 p.m. Very tired. She woke up and sat on her shins instead of W-sit most of the evening. She did not have to catch herself with her hands while sitting. Just pulled herself back with her trunk. She gathered cards with her left hand while holding some cards already in the same hand.

April 16 - Balance does not seem to be any better. She is still up on her knees sometimes though. Two times today when I held Julia and her legs were around my waist, I heard her hip pop, or I think it was her hip.

April 17 - Julia lies pretty still now while pressures are done. Finally, we had a decent morning, but I don't think I am seeing as much progress this time as the last. I think I was expecting too much or I do not know what to expect. Julia said, "I'm ready to go," while she put her hand on her chest. She lay on her side like a relaxed person would. She used her right pointer finger to push a button.

April 18 - Julia woke up this morning and said, "Puppy get me." She remembered her dream. I said, "There is no puppy here. That puppy was just in a dream." She replied, "The puppy bit me.," "Where did he bite you?" "Right here," she said while patting her chest. Later, I tried to get Julia to do a tall-knee walk to the side, but she kept getting down and crept to the other side of the couch. She had no concept of that type of mobility with her legs. Julia pulled on the high chair tray after her trunk had extended and she pulled herself back up to a better sitting position. She had a natural side sitting position with her arm bracing her up. She is remembering things that happened at least two months ago. And she asks many more questions all the time.

April 20 - I'm missing Emily. My husband says she is busy and rarely says much about us. I worry about Emily because of the attention I give to Julia to help her. Julia moved one of her knees forward while tall kneeling, which she had never done before. Signs are showing Julia's function is better than any prognosis any doctor would give her. There are so many times I wish to tell everyone in the world about this special place we found that helps kids. But it is so different and unusual that, when I share it, I get blank stares. They just do not understand. Maybe they think we are grasping at something that will fail. A question I've heard more than once: "Why wouldn't everyone know about this already if it was so great?"

April 21 - Progress on tall kneeling with balance is getting better. I'm so glad the other family came down with us so we were not here by ourselves. I look forward to seeing our bridge going home. I'll probably cry like I did last time.

April 22 - It was so good to hear from Emily last night on the phone. She talked talked talked. I could not get a word in edgewise. What a joy she is! And truly how much I love her. I know I am missing two fun weeks with her. I can't wait to hug and kiss her a lot. We also received a letter today from our insurance stating that they would pay for ALL physical therapy through May 1 of this year. Thank God! I had to see it to believe it. This has been the most stressful time. Finally, we have a letter with proof.

April 23 - Part of the treatment is giving deep pressure to specific areas of the spine, arms, and legs. In the evening, Julia was trying to give deep pressure to Amber. Amber is about a year younger than her. Emily and I played a phone game about what she does well, and later I asked Julia what she did well today, and she said therapy.

April 24 - Julia played while in the tube during treatment, and Barb told someone, "She is so cute!" And then Julia said, "I am something else!" Her character and personality were shining! Verbal language has improved with appropriate comebacks! Chuckling, we left for home around 2:30 p.m. and arrived very late. There were little comments from her throughout.

April 25 - Julia did her exit evaluation at home for Ed, which means I videotaped her and sent it to him to review. We did some errands this afternoon (ate lunch with Amy and went to the bank). At home, the girls played in the sandbox their wonderful daddy made while we were away. Emily and Julia loved it. Emily is a wonderful, loving child. We are so blessed. Julia can now sit on the concrete, bend over, and fill her bowl with sand. She could not do that last summer. I tried to show her how to scoop it, but she said, "No, I'm going to do it this way!"

The girls spent the rest of the afternoon together and swung, rode their Barbie jeep, watched Barney tapes, and ate pickles for snacks. The weather was perfect, everyone was home, and I was thankful for such a peaceful, joyous day!

"He who started a good work in you, will carry it out onto completion until the day of Christ Jesus." (Philippians 1:6)

"Rejoice in the Lord always: and again I say, Rejoice." (Philippians 4:4)

CHAPTER 8

WE WERE GIVEN A hypothesis from Ed that Julia would walk ... in two years. We sure hoped he was right! Yes, it was something we were working toward so that Julia would be able to live a more normal life, but it was also something she wanted for herself. She had been mentioning it quite a bit lately, even putting her shoes on her hands and saying, "I'm walking!" I was happy she had the desire to walk, but it was heartbreaking every time, so having a two-year target was very positive news and spurred me forward.

It was also a relief to have a timeline because it made the problems with insurance feel more manageable. We had just received a letter from our health insurance company. My heart was pounding out of my chest with anticipation because we thought the letter would be similar to the one we had gotten after Julia's surgery in that her treatment costs would be 100% covered. But instead of a letter, I found a bill in the envelope. Insurance was only covering 20%.

Immediately I made a call to the Missouri Department of Insurance for assistance. Since I had a letter stating the insurance company would pay for ALL physical therapy until the following year, I was confused. But after multiple calls, the company wouldn't budge, saying it had to deem the physical therapy "necessary" to cover it all. When I read this, I knew I was about to climb a mountain.

I was adamant that the therapy *was* necessary, explaining that her progress from CCDT was much better than the results she experienced from traditional therapy. I bugged them some more about it until they decided to send the claims to an outside private physiologist to obtain another opinion. Unfortunately, it didn't change anything. I wondered if the medical insurance reviewers and policymakers would really make the same decisions if they were in my position. I know I wouldn't.

My heart really felt I could win this since we had documentation, so I contacted an attorney in case he could help. He referred us to Federal Human Services for legal aid and gave us a phone number. It was a dead end. Literally a dead phone number. So I called another attorney, and he took our case. I sent all the necessary documents to him: claims, letters, our policy. He began creating the case, but it took time because every health care facility we needed additional information from or to clear up discrepancies took weeks and months to get back to us. It was all a waiting game. And in the meantime, the bills were growing. It seemed like all I was doing in my spare time was formulating letters and making phone calls.

At this point, I was not only frustrated but despairing, and uneasy. Other parents had heard about Julia's progress and were asking questions ... including how we were paying for it. I wanted them all to try out CCDT for their children, but I also knew I needed to be honest and explained that we were still fighting with insurance to get coverage. The upside was that Ed was working with us financially until we were able to settle the issues.

As we navigated our finances, another positive was that my husband and I were able to refinance our home for 10 years fixed at 6.875%. This was a huge deal when it came to our payments. We started at 10.5%!

My JCPenney store manager had also made an announcement. Each year, the company worked with a United Way campaign to raise funds for communities and families in need. We met one day as a staff to learn more about the campaign, and my boss said, "This year we would like to use these funds to help Marilyn's daughter, Julia, attend her needed treatment, and I will match whatever amount is raised. Who better to receive a donation than one of our own here in the store?"

I was shocked, humbled, speechless, and grateful. Our family was usually the one that helped others, not the other way around. And our store manager had never matched the funds before. I wasn't used to receiving such kindness and felt overwhelmed. And when they told me the final amount, I nearly cried. The store's associates had raised over $3,000. *$3,000?! All for my baby!* Now we could afford Julia's next trip to the clinic.

Words could not have expressed my profound gratitude, but I did my best and wrote a thank you note to everyone. It hung on our company bulletin board for many weeks, and I would stop to read it again during quiet moments in the evenings to remind me of the goodness in the people I worked with and in the world as a whole. It brought tears to my eyes every time.

Unfortunately, all of our financial problems weren't solved after this act of generosity. It seemed like the incoming good and bad news in that area of our lives was like all the rest: a roller coaster with a lot of highs and lows.

While one employer was raising money for us, my husband's company was dropping the most important part of our insurance needs. They had decided to take away physical therapy from their policy, even though it was known that one of their employee's family members needed it. We felt like we had been stabbed in the back.

We also waited for months to find out if the insurance would pay more than the 20% they had stated for our previous bills, and we finally received a letter in September. It had gone up to 62%. We were thankful, but this was a far cry from 100%. The denial was still based on the specific wording in Julia's evaluation from the clinic, but the insurance company continued to nitpick, finding any small reason not to pay.

Futures Unlimited worked to rewrite Julia's notes from her previous visits so insurance would accept them, but the back and forth took time. So much time that I had to write another letter to the insurance company:

Dear Mr. --------,

Please allow for the extension to file physical therapy claims for Julia to Futures' Unlimited in July and November 1993.

We were told over the phone by a customer service representative, ---------------, that we had the entire year of 1994 and not one year from the date of service. Therefore, we were in no hurry, however, we filed them by the end of 1994.

You had spoken with ----------- at Futures' Unlimited in late January about this claim problem and had asked her to tell me that we could write a letter of extension and that you would personally fix the matter for us. We appreciate your help in extending coverage.

Sincerely, Marilyn

From there, I used my frustration and anger with insurance to write letters to the State Division of Insurance, the State Legislature, Congress, Senators, and even the President (Bill Clinton at that time). I knew it was "little me" against a huge bureaucratic wall and only received a few canned responses. None of them gave me hope that insurance policies or legislation would change. I felt defeated. So, I turned to nonprofits.

My letter to United Cerebral Palsy read:

Dear -------------,

We have applied for services with the Phoebe Valley and Rolla Regional centers to apply for the Stipend program.

Our daughter Julia obtains physical therapy services from Futures Unlimited in Columbus, MS. We would like to apply for travel and lodging funds to help defray the costs of at least one of our trips this year. One trip costs over $1,000. We need all the help we can get as our insurance will be used up at the end of this year. We have 30 days left of physical therapy payments, but we are requesting an extension.

Julia is a bright little girl with a lot of potential. Julia has acquired functions never dreamed of before we started this program. Well, as you can tell, we believe this is the best program for her wellness and will do anything for her future.

Please help Julia continue the trips to this program and increase her body awareness and function. We appreciate any funds you can provide for her.

Sincerely, Marilyn

United Cerebral Palsy did send us a check, and other agencies like Easter Seals supported us at various times as well after I shared Julia's story with them. Although the generous gifts from nonprofits never paid for all of our costs, they kept us afloat. More importantly, they kept Julia in therapy.

"Consider it pure joy, my brothers and sisters, whenever you face trials of many kinds." (James 1:2)

CHAPTER 9

MONTHS FLEW BY AND turned into one year and nearly two. We had stayed busy yet usually stuck to our routines because of Julia's therapy. I continued to keep a daily journal about the small and big life moments of the girls, especially Julia's improvements. I read through some of the entries at the end of 1994 and was blown away by her progress.

There have been changes with her ...

Eyes: Julia first started dramatically crossing her eyes and then rubbing her right eye to get it uncrossed. One night I even watched her pull her right eye inward and then shake her head very hard. After that it seemed like Julia would cross her eyes on purpose sometimes because she would make a face while doing it.

She crossed them at lunch one day, and I asked her what she was doing. "I am crossing my eyes!" Then she proceeded to do it again. I *thought* she was doing it on purpose! She looked at her Grandma another day and said, "Look at my eyes," then crossed her right eye down to the center of her eye socket. *Perhaps her eyes will converge someday*, I noted.

Torso: We used to place a bolster-type plastic device between Julia's legs while she was eating. This would keep her posture upright so she wouldn't slide down in her clip-on chair. But that became no more when she started sitting up by herself with a hand on the table and letting go of it briefly and when she started sitting up in bed with no back support and side sitting. Her torso was holding her up!

There was an afternoon when we were at McDonalds, and I was helping Emily and one of her friends with their food. Before I knew it, Julia had her hamburger and fries out of the bag and was drinking from her cup without spilling anything. And, she was only sitting in a booster chair with minimal side or back support! I hardly knew who she was, she was behaving so independently.

Arms: Julia had the strength of Superwoman. She began by doing pull-ups of sorts on the TV to push the VCR play button before coming back down to a side-sitting position. Then she started pulling herself up with her arms during one of the blue light treatments, which led to her getting onto the therapy table all by herself using her arms. I watched her swing like Tarzan on the swing outside too. She would reach up high and pull on the ropes to pull her entire body up before plopping back down on the swing.

Legs: In the beginning, I would get excited when Julia pulled one leg up toward her face while lying on her back. It was something that babies could do, yet Julia had never been able to do it, but it eventually became a common movement. Then I was excited for Julia to get up onto her knees (called tall kneeling), and she blew me away by staying up on her knees for more than 10 seconds. When her legs stopped scissoring and I'd find her sitting on the school steps independently with her feet flat on the next step down and playing with her shoestrings, I didn't know if it could get any better than that.

But then I watched her begin walking on her knees while tall kneeling! She picked up one knee and moved it forward, then the other, and then back to the first one. Even though her lower leg muscles still felt like they were bound to her bones, her hips, thigh muscles and hamstrings were getting stronger and stronger.

She learned to "stand" while her shins were leaning against a chair. Her feet were on tiptoes, especially her left foot, but she was standing. After that, she would practice springing up onto her feet and holding her balance as long as she could. *Perhaps she will be able to walk someday!*

Sensory Development: Julia had started to get more feeling in her feet. She could feel cold fingers when receiving pressure and would get ticklish too. When she got some mosquito bites, she would ask me to scratch them where she couldn't reach them. She didn't feel the bites before, so this was major for her skin sensory.

Gross Motor Skills: Julia started dressing herself. She would pull her legs up similar to the fetal position and put one leg through one pant hole then the other leg through the other pant hole while pulling the other leg up. It could have been more natural, but she was getting closer. Another time she was half-lying half-sitting and took her jeans off by kicking her legs and moving her jeans with her left hand.

Fine Motor Skills: Even without many occupational therapy treatments, Julia's fine motor skills improved. She was able to put some beans into a small hole and a wooden toy circle into a circle-shaped opening and wooden square into a square-shaped opening. She even used a great pincer grasp and held a pen correctly with her left hand, which led to her switching the pen from the left to the right and making lines next to each other. "There's my name," she said.

Verbal Skills: Originally, Ed had instructed us to use a lamb's nipple to stimulate the back of the tongue and her vomer bone, and I think it worked well. Julia turned into a motormouth! And she was a sassy girl, repeating questions, tattling on her big sister, and becoming very bossy. When she was three years old, she began whining like a typical 3-year-old (which was actually exciting for me to hear). I told her to change her whiney voice to a big girl voice — like a toddler has a big girl voice, ha! — and she did.

Her singing improved too. She had always sung a lot, and it used to sound more like baby babbling ("madagamomobodo"). I would jokingly say she was singing in tongues. Over time, the songs became much clearer, and I would hear the ABCs song, "Old MacDonald Had A Farm," and Barney's "I Love You." It was still jumbled a little but entertaining, and she loved it! *Praise God for her joy!*

Cognitive Skills: Julia came to enjoy playing pretend, even making up her own stories while looking at a book. Her critical thinking had improved too. One day at lunch, I gave her apple slices. She bit into one and said, "Is there apple juice in it?" I thought that was very insightful for a child her age. Another time Amy and Jerry were moving, and she went with her dad to 'help' them. Julia found some screws and nails that were left and began marking up a wall with them. Someone asked, "Julia, should you be doing this to the wall?" Julia replied, "This isn't Amy's house anymore." She thought it was okay because it was no longer her aunt and uncle's. It was very logical ... just not moral!

Social and Emotional Skills: At just three years old, Julia began to feel hurt when her cousins or friends left the room while playing with her because she couldn't keep up with them. It broke my heart. On the flip side, she became skilled at aggravating her sister. For example, she knew Emily wanted to tell me something in the car and started singing very loudly. Emily screamed at her to be quiet, and Julia would laugh knowing she had made her mad. This went on for a while until they worked it out on their own.

While I massaged her ankles one day, Julia said, "Mommy, that feels good. Thank you, thank you!" She even reminded me to say "please" and "thank you" on multiple occasions. *Geez!* And she would say "I love you" or "I missed you" when I got home from work. *So sweet!*

All of the progress in each of these areas was astounding when I looked back on it through my journals. There was no doubt in my mind that CCDT was helping

Julia, and I couldn't have asked for a nicer group of professionals at the clinic. Ed, especially, had always done a great job listening to my questions and concerns and helping me work out any kinks.

For example, after we returned home with a new home program, there was a week or so when Julia didn't want to keep her legs straight out while lying on her stomach to receive specific stroking down her legs. Instead, when I began the stroking technique, her legs would spring up into a frog position, and her arms tightened under her chest, her hands clenched by her shoulders. More importantly, she wanted to stay there. It was like she was frozen in that position. I couldn't tell if it was her being stubborn, if she really liked the position, or if it was developmental from the treatment.

"Julia, help me allow your legs to come down straight," I would say quietly.

"No," she replied while shaking her head.

"But we have to do this part of the treatment with your legs straight," I explained.

It became quite a tug-of-war. The more I tried to pull them — gently, of course — the more her legs wanted to stay next to her chest. It was like she was stuck in this frog position any time she was in the green light (reptilian time period). After a few days of the same sequence, I thought something needed to change.

I reached out to Jennifer since her daughter Amber was doing a very similar home program. Before I even finished my explanation, she said, "Amber was doing the same thing!"

We were both frustrated because we hadn't been able to perform the treatment as recommended, but we were also amazed that the girls could be so in sync. It *had* to be the treatment.

So, I called Ed. I remember he found it a little comical and said, "Let's change the stroking pattern." And what do you know? After the first treatment with the change, they both quit springing into the frog position. *What the heck?!* It was even clearer after this how much CCDT could affect the body's movements neurologically.

There were definitely times when my mind played tricks on me, though. I would wonder if it was all in my head that Julia was progressing. But then someone who knew Julia (family or teachers) would suddenly combat those doubts. Toward the end of the year, my sister came to visit and told me how amazed she was by Julia's physical improvements and was delighted by how much of a conversationalist she had become. "She's taking after her Aunt Kathy!" I responded playfully.

Snow fell a few days later, and the girls couldn't go to daycare, so I got everyone ready to play outside. The prep took 30 minutes. We trudged through the snow in our winter gear, and the girls began trying to build a snowman, throwing snowballs and rolling around. They were both too cold after about 30 minutes of playing, and I couldn't help but laugh to myself. *Thirty minutes of prep for 30 minutes of playtime.* But it was worth it to see those smiles and giggles and enjoy the fresh air.

The following day we got 14 inches of snow on top of the 7 inches from the day before! The girls and I went outside again. The snow wouldn't stick to make a snowman, the drifts were very hard to walk in, and Julia's gloves wouldn't stay on (frustrating!), but we had fun just the same during the short time we were out there. I cooked fried chicken after we warmed ourselves inside. Then Emily and I played Chutes and Ladders, cleaned up her stamp collection, and read some chapters in Charlotte's Web. Julia spent time fiddling with the cassette player trying to get the tapes in and out correctly before her tube therapy. I watched the neighbor clear our driveway and was grateful for the kindness.

It had been a good year.

"But for you who fear my name the sun of righteousness shall rise, with healing in its wings. You shall go forth leaping like calves from the stall." (Malachi 4:2)

PART 2

CHAPTER 10

"I LIVE IN THERAPY," Julia said one day.

Ugh. That was incredibly hard to hear. But I told her it felt that way for me too. Then I asked, "Can you remember how much more you can physically do since you started CCDT?"

She agreed that it was helping her, so we kept moving forward with the treatment. Sometimes she had to go back a step just to leap forward two steps, and not all days were pretty — some were just downright awful. She cried at times, and I cried with her and without her around too.

We took breaks of 3-4 days when the family was busy, but we couldn't give up. How could we when Julia had already changed so much and hadn't plateaued in her progress yet? How could we when Julia, a four-year-old, had told me on several occasions that she wanted to walk like her 11-month-old baby cousin, Mackenzie?

Watching other children grow naturally was difficult. Even though I loved them, was happy for them, and it was a joy to watch my Goddaughter, Mackenzie, grow up, I still felt a sting in my heart for a while. I knew my own child struggled, and it was especially hard when Julia made the comparison herself.

It was painful to continue therapy, holding out hope for progress. But in some ways, it was even more painful to think about stopping — to imagine letting go of that hope."

Lord, give me strength!

I didn't want to regret anything during those development years, though I knew the therapy was taking a toll on Julia. It was taking a toll on the rest of us as well. My husband and I weren't spending time with each other, and I was starting to feel further and further from his heart no matter if I was at the clinic in Mississippi or at home. Emily was also lashing out more and more at Julia.

At the time, I thought it was just kids being kids, but I'm sure she was getting tired of feeling like she was thought of secondly. I didn't want to ignore her, though I was kind of in denial about it; living through each hectic day with the treatment responsibilities gave way to that happening. Time was my enemy.

When Emily wasn't being feisty, she was such a sweet and endearing child, even making up prayers at supper to say something nice about each member of the family. She was also very patient. While Julia was in treatment, Emily had to wait patiently and find something to do by herself. We would try to plan play dates with her friends, and sometimes she would stay in the dim room with us, but the time doing home treatments and our clinic visits in Mississippi caused Julia and Emily's relationship to suffer.

One time when they weren't getting along, I took out one of their dad's old T-shirts and cut the neckhole a little bigger. I made them both put their head in the neckhole, and Emily had her left arm in the left arm hole and Julia had her right arm in the right arm hole. I told them to sit together and love each other, quietly. Initially, they pushed against and groaned at each other, but eventually, I heard giggling.

I smiled to myself. *Maybe we'll all be okay.*

As the two-year mark got closer and closer, Ed mentioned that some families choose to dim most of the home to speed up the progress. I love light, and our house had four large tall windows facing south that allowed the sunshine to pour in. The extra light was especially important in the wintertime to me, so this was a difficult decision. But that February, we covered all of the windows with black plastic, except for the ones in Emily's bedroom and our bedroom.

We did take short breaks from the darkness during the day, and after a while, our eyes became accustomed to the dim light. Unbelievably, we lasted six weeks.

This was longer than what I thought we would make it to, but we were all glad when I finally took the plastic down. Even though Julia made a lot of progress in this period, I could never do it again. There was a suppression of spirit when living in so much darkness; we all needed sunlight.

Life went back to normal for a while, and spring arrived. But in April, Julia woke up with a slight fever and had a dazed facial expression, so I took her to the doctor's office. He said she could be having petit mal seizures, which can be fairly common for children with cerebral palsy. If it continued, the doctor wanted to do an EEG and possibly prescribe some medication. We left the office for home, me worrying that something like this could happen again and Julia repeating in a song rhythm, "I can't breathe, I can't breathe." I didn't understand why she was saying it because she *could* breathe.

For weeks afterward, despite normal EEG results, Julia mostly wanted to remain in the fetal position during treatments. We skipped a day or two of therapy when she started to complain of a headache and stomachache, and I would cuddle her instead. Then she started crying when the blue light was on and I was touching her back with oil. I finished the blue and moved quickly through to the green light. She continued to cry. I turned the blue one back on again. I asked her questions, and she wouldn't answer until she nodded her head ("yes") to sleeping in the bean bag.

"Can you say the words?" I asked. She shook her head no, but became calm when she was in the bean bag for another tube session.

I knew she needed another break from home therapy, but breaks were difficult for me. I felt there was only so much developmental time before Julia might not make any more improvements. Plus, the two-year window Ed had given us about her walking was drawing nearer, and I had become doubtful that it would happen. Time was running out. And I wanted her to reach her potential.

But later that week, Julia said something ... disturbing. It was so alarming, I knew it was time.

We took a break.

"So do not fear, for I am with you; do not be dismayed, for I am your God. I will strengthen you and help you; I will uphold you with my righteous right hand."

(Isaiah 41:10)

"He gives strength to the weary and increases the power of the weak."

(Isaiah 40:29)

CHAPTER 11

WE TRAVELED WITH ANOTHER mom, Lucy, and her daughter, Sandy, who was close to my age, during our next trip to Futures Unlimited. They lived just 2 miles down the road from the home where I grew up, and they attended our church as well. Sandy required more care than Julia, so on this trip, I drove while Lucy tended to Sandy's needs. It was refreshing to have another adult friend travel with me as our conversations made the drive go by faster. There were a few key changes that came from this clinic visit.

First, I learned about another alternative treatment from Lucy: a more natural way of living. She introduced us to a doctor from California who used iridology and did muscle testing to determine what herbs and homeopathic medicine patients needed for healing. I booked an appointment for the girls to see how he could help us the next time he came to Missouri. I didn't know much about this type of care but thought, *Why not?! It can't hurt.*

I don't remember exactly what he said about either of the girls' health, except he did get us started using vitamins for their preventative care and natural antibiotic products for their colds and ear infections. It was very interesting to learn about the options outside of pharmaceuticals.

And, I will never forget how he helped me. His iridology assessment showed that I had stomach issues, and he wanted to see if I had a hiatal hernia since I had given birth to two babies in 15 months. After getting my permission to put his hands on my stomach area, the doctor began gently and slowly pulling and manipulating my stomach tissue down. This lasted for 20 minutes. When he finished, I stood up slowly. Instantly, it was as if I finally had circulation to my head/brain, my stomach was relaxed, and I could stand up straighter much more easily. I felt so good and thanked him over and over again.

From then on, we went to the regular doctor's office to receive a diagnosis for our symptoms but used natural products to combat them. We also found a naturopathic doctor, Dr. Marvin Shipman, a little closer to home in Arkansas and would visit him on occasion. The first appointment we ever booked with him is still so vivid in my mind because he asked me if I was saved.

I was taken aback by the question, and confused. I thought we were there for natural health treatments, and I didn't even know what "saved" meant except that it probably came from a Protestant ideology. Even though I was Catholic, I hadn't been taught that. I hesitated before replying, "I don't know, but I guess I am."

Dr. Shipman must have understood my uncertainty and asked if he could take me through questions and professions of faith. He also explained that this is why he uses the Holy Spirit to help him make decisions about what each client truly needs to heal.

At first I thought it all was very strange, but Dr. Shipman impressed me after we all experienced better health results because of his testing and product recommendations. So, we continued to either call or visit him in Arkansas when our schedule and finances allowed or a need arose.

The second more significant change that occurred because of our most recent trip to Futures Unlimited was to Julia's home therapy regimen. Ed had spent extra time with Julia experimenting with some different movements in the blue light. After that, he added weights to her treatment. Although I noticed they might be stabilizing her when I strapped the weights on Julia's ankles at home, they were also making her legs stronger and stretching her hamstrings. She could move her legs in positions she had not been able to do. Her adductors were also more relaxed.

We worked very hard on basic crawling, during which she couldn't stop talking and I had to ask her not to say anything 35-50 times because when she talked she stopped paying attention to crawling. She would get frustrated and quit, sometimes even cry. She had gotten so used to crawling quickly that her movements were reflexive. Her speed was especially evident when she would get in trouble. I'd watch her crawl away from me as fast as she could to avoid discipline. But the new weights slowed her down and forced her to move more intentionally. Eventually, she could keep them on for about four hours total, and this created more muscle sensations and strength.

We started using blue light a lot more during her tube time and other therapies. One day, we were in blue light and I was giving Julia light touch with tassels while on the oil table. During this treatment, there were intermittent rest times that lasted 10 seconds. Of course, we were fairly good at keeping the talking to a minimum during her therapy and my mind couldn't help but wander. I began by thinking about how warm the room was and if it was just right for treatment. *I wonder what degrees the room is?*

Suddenly, Julia spoke. "Eighty-five to 90 degrees."

I was stunned. *How could she know that? I know I didn't speak my thoughts out loud!*

Some seconds later, I started daydreaming again, and I lost my place in the sequence.

What's next? I asked myself.

Again, I heard Julia speak. "Light touch to the tummy."

OH WOW! I can't believe she did it a second time!

I said nothing to her so the treatment wouldn't be disturbed, but I was giddy inside. In fact, I was getting that feeling in my chest like when you want to laugh but don't because you're trying to make everyone around you think everything is normal? Really, though, you want to burst? That feeling!

However, I calmed myself down to continue the treatment and thought for sure it couldn't happen three times in a row. But ... SHE DID IT AGAIN!

I wonder if I should use mineral oil instead of olive oil.

"Mineral oil," Julia said.

This time, I couldn't help myself. "OH. MY. GOD!"

"What?" Julia asked with surprise. I explained what had just happened. She didn't know why she said what she did, so we both were astonished and giggled. After a little while, we went forward with the next step in treatment, but I couldn't help but think, *What is happening? How could she know what I was thinking? Who do I have here, God? Is this the beginning of something I know nothing about? What is in her future?* It was quite wild, amazing, unbelievable, and something I will never forget!

"He performs wonders that cannot be fathomed, miracles that cannot be counted."

(Job 5:9)

CHAPTER 12

BESIDES A FEW SURPRISING home therapy experiences, CCDT was beginning to feel quite normal to Julia and me. I no longer saw it as an "alternative treatment," per se; it was just a treatment like any other, except that it could also provide some big benefits to people. All of Julia's positive results made me want to share, even proclaim, CCDT with anyone who would listen.

That summer I was getting ready to give a speech to some Girl Scouts at the Lake of the Ozarks. They were learning about a careers badge, and I had been asked by Toree, one of the leaders, to share my experience as a mom of a disabled child.

Toree was an outstanding babysitter for the girls, so we knew her very well. She would bake cookies with them or bring crafts for them to do or make homemade ice cream using coffee tins. I could always count on her to be attentive and caring.

The Girl Scouts group Toree was in charge of was a different audience than I was used to, but for the first time, I wasn't nervous. Plus, having shared Julia's story and how alternative treatments were benefiting her on several occasions before (with other parents and teachers), I had finally gotten used to the fact that not every parent and teacher would care about alternative therapies. And, not every family member, friend, parent or teacher would think I had made the best choice for Julia.

My first encounter with this was when I had been asked to explain CCDT to a small group of parents at the Special Learning Center. Julia was only three, and I had accepted the opportunity with excitement and determination because I was ready to change the world one family at a time.

As I talked, however, although the parents appeared interested, they didn't understand how the therapy could help. I noticed some of their blank facial expressions and became frustrated by my miscommunication and the lack of acceptance. I ended with, "It is very different." Then Debbie Hamler, the director, asked me questions to assist me in describing the treatment. I was relieved she had chimed in, and it helped, but I still felt it was not a successful meeting.

I talked to Ed afterward about the disappointing encounter. He was encouraging and consoled me with the statement, "If it does not have bells and chrome on it, no one wants to listen."

He also mentioned that if it could be organized, he would travel up to Missouri to meet with even more parents and put together a mini educational conference for them. I was so surprised and grateful he was willing to do that but even more grateful that Debbie was on board with the idea, so we set the date. I was asked to speak again during it, but this time only about Julia's specific treatments and how it had helped her.

Although I can't remember exactly what I said, I did go over the progress Julia had made and the benefits that came after each visit to Futures Unlimited, which I was always elated to share. This was my outline for the speech:

First Visit:

- Happier

- Balanced better

- Better arm control; reached with both arms up at the same time

- Lifted toys while W-sitting from one side to the other or in front of her

- Improved speech; sentences arrived

- Creeped better

Second Visit:

- Improved in all the areas mentioned in the first visit

- Started to tall kneel all by herself

- Spoke emotional sentences about feelings she had

- Mimicked wonderfully

- Got to a sitting position all by herself from a lying position

- Took a large tank top shirt off by herself

Third Visit:

- Sat with a straighter back while side sitting; used no hands for support

- Sat in her chair without a blue bolster between her legs to keep her from extending out of the chair

- Started conversations; told on her sister; pretended by herself

- Stayed up on her knees, tall kneeling, longer than ever and began to function while up (for example, pressed buttons and played with toys)

I was also vulnerable and honest, explaining that there were emotional logistics to conquer that I didn't even realize when we began down this path. I had to cross a line from traditional to alternative, which meant taking the chance that people wouldn't accept my decision and might judge me in respect to being a competent mother. I had to walk away from what the majority of other families do, and it was difficult because there was not much support to begin with and there would be fewer conversations for support. I also did most of the treatments, took notes, and traveled long distances to help my daughter more than what was typical.

"But I chose this treatment for Julia because I felt there was no better choice, especially after seeing her progress," I explained. "Julia improved more than she ever did when doing traditional treatments, so I couldn't go back to the old ways … My reason for being here this evening is to help other parents understand this therapy that can help their children. I'm not here to tell you that I'm right and you are wrong or this is better than your way, but my heart wants to help you try something new for your child to see how they could improve. And I hope you will do it."

I felt like the talk went well, and even if many of the parents didn't try the clinic, I knew that was okay too. It was no longer about me going on a crusade to change people's minds or turn them to CCDT after one speech, but I was satisfied to just share when possible. Then I hoped and prayed for the other children as well and thanked God that He gave me the treatment to help Julia.

And that was how I went into the Girl Scout meeting — passionate and grateful. I was in my element; I had no plan, but the words simply flowed out of me.

I talked about Julia, who she was and what she was like. I spoke about not limiting yourself to finding what traditional medicine has to offer in terms of healing because it may not have all the answers. I shared about the therapy we found at Futures Unlimited and the difference between the progress of the therapies.

I explained the challenges kids like Julia face with the public school system regarding what they will and will not provide. I encouraged them to accept all children and adults no matter what they see on the outside. To look beyond the disability.

The Girl Scouts leader, Toree, was very pleased with the talk, and as I drove home, I was at peace. I knew I would always share Julia's journey with others in case it might help them, and that I would always advocate for the life my daughter deserved. Maybe I wasn't changing the world yet, but I was changing my little corner of it, which would have to do for now.

"So let's not get tired of doing what is good. At just the right time we will reap a harvest of blessings if we don't give up." (Galatians 6:9)

"So don't be anxious about tomorrow. God will take care of your tomorrow too. Live one day at a time." (Matthew 6:34)

CHAPTER 13

JULIA WAS ABOUT TO graduate from the Special Learning Center. She would have the opportunity to start school in the fall, which meant I needed to figure out what services would be provided for her over the summer. When I called the school, the news wasn't good: there "wasn't enough funding" to continue Julia's therapy program with her aides, Tami and Julie.

It was ridiculous! The aides only did therapy with Julia for four hours a week. *How can they not afford this?*

Around that same time, I attended an Individual Education Plan (IEP) meeting during which a legal document would be created outlining Julia's educational program for the school year. I wasn't sure yet if she would stay home with me or go to public school, but I did want to see what the school would provide.

Julia's aide, Julie, contacted me before the meeting with some insights about parents' rights: 1) I don't have to sign the IEP; and 2) At the meeting, if I didn't agree with the decision, then I should tell them to reschedule in two weeks and give them time to talk to my legal advisor.

The meeting didn't go very well. I disagreed with what they had planned for her education, but what was even crazier was that on the last page of the document, they had included that Julia "preferred to stay with her resident family." The wording was odd, like Julia could choose who to stay with at that age. And I didn't like it. *What if Julia and I were simply having a bad day and she flippantly told her teacher she didn't want to live with her family anymore? Could she be taken away from us? If I signed the IEP, could the government alter every part of her life?*

Needless to say, I wrote an IEP rejection letter. Soon after, I called Missouri Protection and Advocacy Services, and we were placed on its waiting list. We were 21st in line, but when the time came, the board never added our case to its list because the members only voted on adult cases during that term. So that was a lost cause.

I also wrote a second letter about Julia's lack of a summer program.

Dear --------,

In retrospect of Julia's IEP meeting on May 26, we discussed the dilemma of state funding being cut to early childhood intervention and Julia's need for the services that have been provided.

We know that you understand I do Julia's therapy at home consistently. As you also know, we have Julia's sister, Emily, at home this summer too. It is very difficult to provide quality therapy and quality childcare simultaneously.

Our request and compromise to you would be to allow Julie P. to provide Julia's therapy two times a week for 2 hours per day for 6 weeks this summer and discontinue services from Early Childhood Intervention in the fall.

Please reply with an answer as soon as possible as the summer will slip away before we know it. Our summer trip to Futures Unlimited is July 1-15. So, if Julie could provide services for 6 weeks around that time, it would be very much appreciated.

Sincerely, Marilyn

We received a reply that they agreed to allow the six weeks of services over the summer, and I was so grateful. I actually won a small battle! I was behind on a multitude of important life tasks, and Emily was so good that I was able to accomplish most of my projects. I even attended a Pampered Chef party and decided to make the switch from my JCPenney jewelry position to a Pampered Chef consultant. This would allow me to be home more while still making decent money.

We continued to work on Julia's therapy as much as possible, and our next trip to Futures Unlimited was a lot of fun because we decided to use our drive down as a family vacation. We visited Grant's Farm in St. Louis, where we fed some billy goats. We ate at Lambert's Cafe near Sikeston, Missouri; it was fun trying to catch the rolls being thrown at us. Once we arrived in Mississippi, Ed invited us to swim in the pool at his house, which we did before driving to Foley, Alabama, to enjoy the beach, ice cream, and local holiday fireworks. Although it ended up being a long drive, it was a much-needed vacation for us all before Julia started her treatment.

This time Ed implemented several changes for Julia. One was that he wanted her legs in a crisscrossed strap contraption so that it slowed them down and forced them to stay flexed and not extended. I measured the correct length for her size and made the straps out of broadcloth. This method worked well in that she could sit in her rocking chair with her feet beautifully flat, pull herself up to stand at a flexed squat position, and walk with her left foot very flat to the floor and on the ball primarily of her right foot while I held her hands. But Julia tired of the straps eventually, and we went back to the ankle weights.

Sometime after returning from the clinic, I was asked by public school officials to send in a daily journal of what I did while at home. Apparently, they didn't think I was doing Julia's home program. I did comply and made sure to show them every hour of my days: when I did therapy; made breakfast, lunch, and dinner;

did laundry; ran errands; worked on my Pampered Chef business; helped Julia take a bath and brush her teeth; tucked the girls in before bed.

As if making and sending in this list wasn't frustrating enough, a woman from the public school system called to let me know that the department didn't want to provide two to three homebound sessions for Julia anymore.

"You are providing a service that is personalized for every other disabled student there. Why not for my daughter?" I asked.

I then explained that I had proof showing that Julia's first 13 months in traditional therapy had little to no improvement and possibly worsened the spasticity in her feet. I shared more about her progress after doing the passive therapy from Futures Unlimited. "Why would you choose the least beneficial therapy for my child?"

The woman said that this was a different philosophy from what they can provide, and I argued that a neighboring school had been providing this therapy for one of their 11-year-olds. I also added that the school system had been providing the service for the past two years for Julia, so that was proof that it was possible.

"I believe the Department of Mental Health is funding Early Child Development and says it is not educational," said the woman.

"So 'educational' means throwing bean bags over her head for PT?" I responded. "This is in her IEP! PLAYING? WHAT KIND OF SYSTEM DO WE HAVE? I can play with her!!! You can practice, practice, practice all day long, but until she has the motor neurological understanding of her body, she will not be able to do what is requested. They are just wasting her time. I believe one of the teachers at the school knows this is true."

"I understand that the passive therapy has helped your daughter, and I know you want what's best for her," the woman said. "Unfortunately, I feel like my hands are tied. This type of therapy isn't in the policy or regulations to adhere to."

Once again, regulations ruled how our children were taught even though there was evidence that a personalized approach would benefit a student's development and education. Things needed to change. So once I hung up with the woman from the public school system, I called the director of Special Needs Education at DESE and left a message. And I researched what the state and federal laws had to say about it.

Then I wrote a letter to the principal of the school Julia would be attending:

Dear -----------,

Enclosed is a copy of the PL 94-142, which explains the Education for all handicapped children Act. I am sure you have read this in the past. It explains in detail that Julia has the right to a full range of educational services that include physical therapy and more.

We feel we have explained our choice for Julia's passive physical therapy thoroughly in the past, but I will explain it again. Julia had active therapy at the local hospital from 13 months to 26 months of age. In those 13 months, she also had orthopedic surgery. Six months after the surgery, Julia's legs were scissored again, crossing at the knee, and active therapy was not able to alleviate the symptoms of her neurological disorder of spastic diplegia. Actually, by Christmas of 1992, we believed her spasticity in her feet and legs had gotten worse. This was heartbreaking because she went through all that pain, and it did not help her. To have scar tissue from it was even more saddening.

As parents, we knew Julia needed a change because she still could not sit up in her bar chair without sliding to her side. She could not play with toys with both arms independently and/or at a W-sit. She could not side sit, circle sit, creep, tall kneel, or giggle. She had definitive scoliosis. She was not accepting this active therapy that was prescribed by the doctor, and we thought that was the only possible treatment.

However, she experienced therapy at Futures Unlimited in February 1993 intermittently for 30 months. Her accomplishments are as follows from the passive physical therapy she received there:

[I inserted a long list of examples here.]

Julia's progress is exceptional and quite extraordinary and will continue. There are many reasons why Julia needs passive physical therapy, and these are just a few examples of her progress. This is Julia's special need. The PL 94-142 allows Julia to obtain services for her special needs at this point in her life from the public school system.

We do not understand why any public school, or educator, would choose to send professionals to our home to play with Julia, throwing bags over her head while tall kneeling, when active therapy proves mostly unbeneficial.

As my notes above prove, Julia is, however, very progressive with passive physical therapy and it is physically educating our daughter. Each child is special and has specific special needs. Passive PT is Julia's special need for her physical education.

Please call us at xxx-xxxx when we can begin Julia's home programming directed by Futures Unlimited for the fall 1995 school year.

Sincerely, Marilyn

I had hoped this would prove to be a successful letter to an end for Julia's passive therapy. But it was not to be. So as I had always done, I soldiered on through Julia's treatments with some help, but mostly alone.

—ell—

"When you feel weary, know that God's strength is endless. He will renew your spirit and give you the courage to press on." (Isaiah 40:29)

CHAPTER 14

EVERY DAY BEGAN TO feel the same to me. And every day was busy.

I was cooking meals, doing laundry, shopping for what we needed, helping Emily with her homework in the evenings, making Pampered Chef calls and taking care of deliveries, planning for life events or holidays, reading to the girls, calling insurance, reaching out to nonprofits for financial help, journaling, and playing with the girls outside when the weather was nice.

These were the tasks of every parent in America, yet I was also squeezing therapy into the schedule whenever possible — before and after events and meetings, between household chores, while Emily was at school or with friends. And I was doing it all pretty much by myself ... with, what felt like, the world against me.

I was spreading myself too thin, and it was taking a toll. My inner drive wasn't there and neither was the necessary get-up-and-go feeling. I was tired and wanted to do nothing. But no matter how hard I tried, I could not stop with any of it.

I wondered what the future held for Julia: if therapy was still making a difference, if she was happy, and if she would ever be treated like everyone else. Even though we were close to our extended family and they had been very supportive and loved Julia, her cousins didn't always include her in games and other activities, even those she could take part in, because it took too much patience to wait on her or they would have to alter the rules so that she could play. Every time this happened, I had to watch Julia's little face fall and sadness fill her eyes. Sometimes Emily was excluded as well because it meant then Julia would need to be asked to join, and that was upsetting for her too.

I wasn't able to be with Emily as much as I wanted either, and it was breaking my heart. She was good at playing with others and was still being so nice to her sister. At school one day she even drew a picture of what she was thankful for, and it was of Julia. How can she be so kind despite everything else going on? The thought made me want to cry.

My husband and I were also moving in opposite directions geographically, spiritually, emotionally, physically. There was one day in particular when it felt like we were in a "no-win situation."

It was a Sunday, and I had gotten up late. My husband and I argued, went to church and acted like everything was okay, and came home just to argue some more. I cried before putting Julia in the tube. *I hate my life! Why do I have to succumb to showing so much emotion just to get him to listen? Am I the only one who cares? I feel like I'm doing everything for this family by myself!*

He might have felt that way too since he was the full-time breadwinner. But if he was feeling the same way as me, I wouldn't have known it because he rarely communicated. He didn't want to listen to what I wanted and needed for our family: more time together. One weekend we did go camping at Bennett Springs, but while my husband was fishing, everything was proving to be a frustration for me. I tried to play with Emily at the camp and include Julia, but the wooded and rugged environment hindered her from moving well. So after that trip, I decided it was not fun for the girls and me, and we never went again.

I wanted to give my husband grace. After all, I wasn't able to give him very much attention because I was focused on the girls, and he was doing extra work to help pay for everything. But though I was married, I felt very alone. Days and weeks continued to pass. It was as if a dark cloud was always hanging above my head.

I began planning the next trip to Futures Unlimited, and a little bit of the sadness dissipated. I would never admit it, but I always looked forward to going. Besides the possibility of Julia's improvements, the trip had turned into a retreat from the mundane parts of my life. It was my respite from doing Julia's treatment, and it opened up some free time for myself, which usually turned into running necessary errands and picking up items for the girls.

The only downside to the trips to the clinic was that Emily wasn't there. I called her almost every night. One evening she would be sad because she missed me, and the next she would be busy at her grandma's house and didn't want to take the time to talk. I bought her some clothes while I was out shopping and collected pine cones outside our trailer after she said she needed some for a school project. I wanted her to know that she was loved and that I was sad because I missed her too.

On the last day of therapy before going home, I decided to meet with Ed ... about me. We had developed a professional friendship, and I hoped he could assess me. He said he could do some eye coordination testing.

I held a pen in front of my face with my arms straight out and moved my hand in circles while one eye followed my fist in a circle. The other one was covered. Then I held the pen without a stretched arm and moved it in a circular motion while following it with one eye at a time. He also watched how I crawled.

Afterward, Ed said he believed I could be suppressing something sub-dominantly because I did not go in a full circle with the pen in my left hand while using my left eye. "It is not developed," he said. "Your brain hasn't allowed itself to think about whatever it is you are suppressing. Perhaps you're thinking too much too constantly."

He added, "And be aware: people who have a lot to think about can be on the verge of depression."

I sighed but laughed to myself. *I guess that's no surprise.*

Ed suggested I listen to 40s and 50s music and look at color and circular art to help finish out the circle, so I went to the music store nearby to see if they had a tape with songs from those decades, but they did not. I decided to visit another music store when I got home, and I made a note about a book Ed recommended that discussed herbs to improve health and wellness.

For the first time, I also experienced six days of the treatment at the clinic.

I had always had a rounded back, which was hereditary from my dad. I couldn't straighten it without pain, and in a couple of seconds, I would give in and slump again. When I was about 11 years old, my mom found a back brace to help hold my shoulders back, but it felt like a straight jacket. By the second day, I had screamed, "Get this off me! Take it off! I can't breathe!" And my mom relented and helped me remove it.

Now, after years dealing with a curved back, Ed thought his treatment could help me. I experienced all of the same treatments as Julia and the other patients. One day while I was in the tank with ferns over it and in green light, I began to feel very paranoid and claustrophobic. I started to breathe deeper and faster and asked to get out. It was a really weird feeling. However, I continued with the six days of treatment, and once I was finished, my back felt much better. I could even breathe more easily! It seems I had been living in a straight jacket after all and didn't realize it.

After I returned home, my husband said, "Ed saved your life." It was an amazing transformation and healing that allowed me to live with a straight back without pain.

This was the beginning of my focus on more significant self-care since becoming a mom. Prioritizing myself was essential to take good care of my girls. I knew this to be true, yet it had become so difficult over the past several months, and maybe even years. So, I began calling Kathy and Amy more often when I was in a slump. They became my rocks and sounding boards.

My other sister-in-law, Sharon and Amy, too, were generous with her time and kept the girls when they could to give me a break for work, and I watched their children too; at times, it seemed as though we were playing musical houses. I also met with other moms for playdates for the girls and started walking or jogging in the early mornings with a friend two to three times a week, which improved my mental and physical state.

I once heard someone say, "After you marry, keep your girlfriends." Thank goodness I had because they helped me through this time of depression. And I knew they would continue to do so because there would be more trials to come. I had decided to keep trying my hardest to take care of my body, journal, rest, and — especially when the days felt too hard — simply do my best. And I would need the reminder from those who loved me that this was enough.

"My brothers and sisters, [1] whenever you face trials of any kind, consider it nothing but joy, 3 because you know that the testing of your faith produces endurance."

(James 1:2-3)

"When the righteous cry for help, the Lord hears and delivers them out of all their troubles. The Lord is near to the brokenhearted and saves the crushed in spirit."

(Psalm 34: 17-18)

Chapter 15

WHILE I WAS TRYING to hold it all together, Emily was feeling disconnected. She had been shuffled around to different family members' houses a bit more than usual due to the trips to the clinic and had begun to show signs that she needed more time with me and our family as a whole. For example, her behavior at school was changing — not for the better — and I received some kind but firm comments in her kindergarten parent-teacher conferences.

Behaviorally, Emily had been a pretty normal kid for a while. A couple years ago, when she was four, there had been some issues, but they were reflections of my parenting choices. At the time, I had brought her with me to Futures Unlimited, and Ed was able to meet her. She moved around quickly and kind of nervously when introduced to this new person. She was also telling me "no" a lot in front of him when I told her not to do something.

Later, Ed told me, "You need to get a handle on this child before she becomes a teenager. Your fights will get much worse."

This had been difficult to hear about my little firstborn princess. In my eyes, she could do no wrong, and I wanted to give her whatever she wanted. But now I was questioning some of my actions and reactions toward her behavior.

For instance, I would usually let her choose which color of cup she wanted from the cabinet. She would pick, say, green, and I would get it down for her.

"No, I want pink!" she'd say. And then I'd grab the pink.

No sooner would I fill up the pink cup with juice or whatever she was drinking when she'd say, "I want yellow!" or that she wanted something else to drink. Yes, it was a bit annoying, but I'd change it for her every time until she was satisfied.

Apparently, this is a big mistake in parenting ...

When Ed showed me that I needed a firmer hand with Emily (I didn't spank my kids, yet), it was eye-opening for me. I certainly understood that she was rebellious like many children at that age and began working on it. Sometimes she didn't want to eat what I prepared for meals, and I finally got so frustrated one evening that I took her plate, walked downstairs to the dog food bag, and proceeded to put a little pile of dog food on her plate.

I stamped loudly back up the stairs and put her plate in front of her. "Here, eat this if you don't want to eat what I made!"

Now, I would have never let her eat dog food, but I wanted Emily to understand that I wasn't going to budge when it came to what she ate for dinner.

Julia started to giggle when she saw the dog food. Emily gave her a stern look. She was not happy at all. But after she stared at the pile of nuggets and then observed me standing firm, she decided the food I prepared would be fine and begrudgingly ate it anyway.

Later, the girls would laugh about that moment and could still hear the dog pellets dropping onto the plate. But at that point, I was frustrated and determined that my four-year-old wasn't going to win the food war. And thanks to Ed's direction, she didn't.

Of course, we had other battles, but having created new boundaries as a parent, I found that Emily soon became much easier to manage. So it was concerning when her kindergarten teacher told me she wasn't behaving as well as she had been. I knew I needed to make more of an effort to be with her whenever possible.

We still read books in the evenings, but I also was room mother *and* began helping lead her Girl Scout troop despite my lack of extra time. We did many activities together to earn her badges, which I would sew onto her vest. She was my little assistant and helped me pass out the "try-it" patches to the other girls, we went to the Girl Scout Brownie Zoo Day, we sold cookies (it wasn't a highlight for either of us!), and we attended the Girl Scout Investiture.

In December, Emily had a part in the school Christmas program, so I curled her hair, which the other kids oohed and aahed over. She did a fantastic job singing a solo in her shaggy and brown donkey costume, and she looked so beautiful. I was beyond proud!

During snow days, we would spend the whole day together playing games, putting together puzzles, and watching movies. It warmed my heart to hear Emily say she "had a good day at home."

She came with us on our next trip to Futures Unlimited too. We worked on her schoolwork in the morning while Julia was in therapy. We played cards, took short walks since it was cold, and shopped a little. Unfortunately, the pipes froze in our trailer, so we had to move to another one in order to shower, cook and stay warm in the unusually subzero windchill, but we made the most of it.

"I am the firstborn, and Julia is the second," Emily said randomly one evening.

"That's right." I nodded and smiled.

"But she can't walk," Emily continued, "and that makes her very special."

I abruptly stopped what I was doing. *Does she feel like Julia is more special than her?* I wondered. Then I did my best to combat those thoughts and fears she might have and tried to explain to her that we are all special in our own way. I hoped she understood and also hoped that bringing her along to Julia's treatment was showing her how special I thought she was. I didn't want her to feel excluded, unwanted, or more importantly, unloved. But I still wasn't sure how to balance it all to make it all okay.

Before we left the clinic at the end of the two weeks, Ed offered to briefly assess Emily's development too and gave me her own home program, which included using large flashcards, drawing shapes with wide markers, and doing some physical exercises. I also asked him what he thought about the education system and what would be best for Emily because I was wrestling with the decision to switch Emily from regular school to homeschooling. I had been on several phone calls with other parents who were also considering homeschooling their children or who had switched to homeschooling already. They thought it had allowed their children to become more mature.

Ed agreed with this outcome. He believed the education system was often too politics-driven and was not able to teach each child as they individually needed. Keeping Emily at home for first grade could allow her brain to figure out subdominant and dominant, create less pressure and stress, and give her better confidence and higher self-esteem. He was all for it.

What he said made sense to me too, and I was excited about the chance to accelerate her learning. The cons of homeschooling Emily, though, had to do with social skills and the possibility of boredom at home since there were fewer kids around.

I mulled over the decision for weeks after my conversation with Ed. It wasn't an easy one because though I would see Emily more, it would be as her "teacher," and homeschooling would add even more responsibility to my daily routine. But in the end, I decided to homeschool her, and she seemed fine with it. In fact, she quickly began planning out her own days, even writing me a letter asking if she could stay up later, which made me chuckle. I told her that was okay as long as we came up with a different bedtime together and she stuck to it.

I also picked up some homeschooling curriculum books from the library and began making plans for her lessons at home. Here's what I wanted Emily to learn:

- Math: flashcards for up to 10+; work to triple digits addition and carrying 1-digit and 2-digit additions; understand inches with a ruler; measure in food volumes to cook; greater and lesser than 99; counting by 2s, 3s, 5s, 10s and 100s.

- Science: nature walk to the back of our land to observe and compare seasons in notebooks; understand our relationship with the world

- Social Studies: read books about other people in other countries

- History: learn about major events and how they have changed the world

- Geography: look at maps, etc.

It was an ambitious curriculum, but I didn't want Emily to get behind in anything. And I couldn't wait to see how she and I would work together with me as her teacher.

When Emily stopped going to school, she seemed glad to be home, except when she got in trouble. One day Julia and Emily were fighting over something and were disciplined. Afterward, Emily said she was packing up and leaving. "But not to school," she added. She earnestly walked back to her bedroom.

On her way there, I replied, "Well, it's too cold, but if you have to leave ..." I knew she wouldn't go anywhere, but I began to help her anyway.

She decided she would wait for the summer before she left, and I said if she did that then she would miss going with us on the next clinic trip. Then she decided she would wait until the fall, but I told her that's when school started again. Upon hearing that, she decided to kiss and hug Julia and tell her she loved her. Julia told her she loved her back, and all was well.

Finally, Emily and I were spending a lot of time together. She started gymnastics, and I got to watch her during practices. We read more and more books, and I had made large flashcards from white cardstock paper for Emily to learn words from the books we had checked out at the library. We went through the cards nearly every day. While she was lying on her belly, I would quickly flip each one three times while I said the word out loud to her. I did about five words in a row, and then we'd go back and review all five, having her repeat each word before moving on to the next set of words. After we finished all of the flashcards, I used our projector to cast the page of the book onto the wall in Julia's bedroom since it was a dim room already, and Emily would read each page to us.

She learned 39 words by sight in just two nights, and we had only worked on them for about 45 minutes altogether. I wasn't sure I'd be able to make enough flashcards to keep up with her. I stayed up late making flashcards at least three nights a week. It was amazing to me how smart she was and how quickly she learned. It was also very rewarding for me since I was part of her progress and could see her success.

We also played Monopoly Junior and card games, drew pictures, made a cardboard house, and continued with all of her Girl Scout events. One highlight was when I went with her and the rest of the Brownie Troop to Camp Pin Oak. The leaders and the girls played games, made crafts, went canoeing, and swam. And in the evening, we sat around a campfire singing songs, roasting marshmallows for s'mores, learning about owls and trying to call them (with no luck).

Emily had even begun helping me with the normal tasks around the house. One day I was at the cooktop making some meat for dinner and asked Emily if she wanted to help.

"Okay," she said.

"Good. Get four potatoes and wash them."

She did.

"Now, poke each potato with a fork so they can be cooked in the microwave," I instructed her.

While I was busy preparing the rest of the meal, I heard the utensil drawer open and some clinking behind me. And then after a while, it was quiet.

"What's next, Mom?" she asked proudly.

I turned around and OMG! Each potato had a fork sticking out of it! I started laughing, hard. It struck me so funny that I had tears rolling down my cheeks! We had been reading *Amelia Bedelia* books together, and it reminded me of something Amelia would do.

But then I looked at Emily, who was not joining in on my amusement. She had done exactly what I told her to do and didn't understand why I was laughing. I had hurt her feelings, and trying to explain about the *Amelia Bedelia* stories didn't help. So, I became serious again and came down to her level. "Oh, Emily, you did exactly what I told you to do." I then showed her what I actually needed done and how I should have explained it better.

I definitely wasn't a perfect parent. But even though it was a hurtful moment for

Emily and a learning experience for me, it was still part of the family memories that I had been craving. We seemed to finally be making them with Emily at home. And it was incredibly rewarding. The girls were more satisfied learning so quickly and doing life together, and I treasured every single moment with them.

"Discipline your children, and they will give you rest; they will give delight to your heart." (Proverbs 29:17)

CHAPTER 16

IT HAD BEEN THREE and a half years since Julia started CCDT therapy, and I was beginning to get a bit discouraged. I had been diligently doing Julia's treatments, even if the time had lessened some when compared to the time we spent on it years before, but it felt as though her progress had slowed. We weren't hitting *my* goals for her. Even after several of her recent trips to Futures Unlimited, there weren't many changes to note, and Julia and I were getting tired of going.

Ed gave me hope. During one talk, he explained a theory he was figuring out that still had some loopholes. I couldn't quite understand it, but it was something to do with an evolutionary sequence of development. He said that when a new development sequence evolved in a patient, it always accelerated a patient's progress. This had kept him going for all these years and was why he continued with his patients' therapies.

But it made me wonder: *Will Julia's abilities continue to evolve with CCDT?* It didn't help that we had gone to an appointment with one of the doctors who had seen Julia years prior, and the only thing she noted was what Julia could NOT do rather than what she could. She totally disregarded any progress Julia had made.

The bills for Julia's alternative treatment kept coming too, and my husband said he was tired of being broke. I asked him what we could do differently as I was already going to garage sales for the girls' clothes and cutting out coupons for groceries in addition to working part time. He told me I could get a full-time job again. "Okay, then you do half the laundry, half the vacuuming, half the therapy, and Emily will need to go back to school," I retorted. He simply turned back to the desk and didn't say anything.

Despite my disappointment regarding Julia's slower progress, I felt thankful. Julia hadn't lost any of the skills she had gained over the years, and I knew she would have never progressed as much as she had with traditional therapy. She was able to do so much more than what was initially expected, and I had watched with pride over the past year as she had become more and more independent.

If her big sissy took her PJs off and threw them into the laundry, Julia did it too. In fact, she wanted to do everything she watched Emily do. So, Julia had learned how to dress herself entirely, though she was still figuring out how to put on her shoes. "I can do everything now, Mom!" she had said excitedly. She could go to the bathroom — even getting herself on and off the potty — and get into bed all by herself.

Her feet were now able to move independently from the rest of her body, which was new, and her hand-eye coordination had improved. She could even play catch with a ball while tall kneeling. One day I watched her sit Indian style, which she had been doing daily, while putting together a 25-piece puzzle. Her balance and weight-bearing while standing was getting better too, and she practiced walking between the couch and the coffee table while holding and putting her weight onto them.

Past her physical capabilities, Julia was stretching her mental abilities as well. She learned to call people on the phone all by herself and to recognize numbers. Her speech had gotten much better during our work together with the flashcards, and she could sing full verses of songs. I also found that she enjoyed being creative with various forms of art. By herself, and with no guidance from anyone, Julia pushed a hole through the middle of a Styrofoam plate, put a straw through the hole, and taped it. Then she told Emily that she had made an umbrella, which was followed by a proud giggle. Totally adorable!

Yet it was still hard for me to watch her with other children her age because it continued to be a reminder of what she couldn't do. Although they generally liked her, during playtime, she couldn't always keep up, so sometimes the kids would quit a game or choose not to play with her, even leaving the room. She would often play by herself or ask me to join, and we would try to play with some of the preschool games but would often have to adjust them so that they would work for her.

She did love books, though, despite the fact that her eyes tired quickly. She was always opening and closing the covers. I wondered if it was because it was something she could do to keep up with the other kids or achieve success. And I knew she needed to have that feeling at times because some days were simply harder than others.

Once, after Emily had returned to elementary school at St. Martins (she was ready to be with friends again), it snowed so much that the school closed. So we all stayed home and went outside to play. As you may remember, it was an ordeal to get dressed for the snow. But we got ready in the usual 30 minutes and went out into the cold.

Not too long after we began playing, Julia had to potty. (And yes, she went before we had gone outside.) I knew it would take 10-15 minutes to carry her inside, have her go to the bathroom, and come back out, and during that time, Emily would be outside playing by herself. AGAIN! I also wanted to avoid some back pain that usually arrived while carrying Julia. So instead, I said, "Will you try to potty outside rather than taking your clothes off inside and getting redressed?"

Just to clarify, we lived on a very quiet street, and Julia was wearing a two-piece snowsuit, so she would only be undressed from the waist to the knees. In my mind, I also thought pulling down her pants like she had done before would be easy. It wasn't.

But my poor child was obedient. I held her up from behind and pulled down her snowsuit bottoms, and then I waited and waited and waited. The struggle of holding her up began to get the best of me, and I noticed Emily rolled her eyes as she watched the unfolding situation.

"Are you done yet?" I asked.

"I'm trying!" Julia replied. Understandably, she was having a hard time in the cold and the snow.

But, finally, she went ... and unfortunately peed on her pants.

Ugh. What was I thinking?

This blunder on my part wasn't funny, though we laughed about it later. I had to carry Julia inside after all to change her, and Emily got cold and probably bored waiting on us. She decided to come inside too. I then tried to make up for it all by cooking chicken noodle soup and warming up some hot chocolate (their favorite).

That snow day was also another turning point because it had become even more apparent that I could no longer carry Julia as easily wherever she needed to go. And so, at age 7, Julia got her first wheelchair. Ed reminded me that once children get a wheelchair, the less they want to be on the floor, and he was right. As the days passed, I watched Julia choose to stay in her wheelchair more and more. I was worried because this inhibited the progression of back strengthening, but on the positive side, it allowed her to be closer to people's level for conversation.

Ed and I also had a brief conversation about looking into another house for accessible reasons. My husband and I had a nice home, but when we originally built it, we had no idea it would need to be accessible. So I searched the newspaper and with a realtor just in case there was a house out there we could afford but quickly realized that we'd have to build one, which just wasn't feasible yet.

However, we were able to purchase a van with an arm lift on the side, and I couldn't wait to use it on our next drive to the clinic. But even the cool van feature couldn't redeem our "trip from hell."

"When the time is right, I, the LORD, will make it happen." (Isaiah 60:22)

CHAPTER 17

FOR SEVERAL YEARS, A dear friend Denise and her son, John, had joined us on our trips to Futures Unlimited. We had met them at the clinic when both John and Julia were just starting treatment. They lived in Iowa, so they would meet us in St. Louis, and we would drive down to Mississippi together. John needed more attention, so it was helpful for Denise to have another driver, and I appreciated having a friend around to drink *very* sweet southern tea with and talk about life with while the kids were in treatment.

But this time, Denise and John didn't carpool with us, and I wasn't looking forward to the long drive without them.

The drive was uneventful until we got south of Memphis and I noticed a small gray Datsun-type truck speeding behind our van and gaining quickly. I was in the left lane, so I moved to the right, allowing the other driver to pass since they were going a good 15 mph faster than me.

Instead, when the truck sped up beside me, it stayed there.

Of course, like anyone, I looked over to see who it was and why they had slowed down. Inside the truck, which was lower to the ground than my van, was a heavy-set man in his 50s who was unshaven and unkept. I could see the beer cans littering his passenger seat. Even worse, to my horror, I could see that his pants were unzipped and he was trying to show off what was underneath. He smirked at me, and I can still remember his bulging eyes.

OH MY GOSH!!! I felt like I needed to wash my eyes out.

I glanced in the back to see if Julia was paying attention, and thankfully, she was playing with a toy and not looking out the window. "Julia, look down!" I said and then quickly realized that was the wrong thing to say because it piqued her curiosity.

"For what?" she said, very confused.

"Just look down," I anxiously replied. Back then, I had a bag cell phone, and the lit numbers on it faced upward while it sat on its cradle. This allowed me to quickly and stealthily dial *55 and waited for a voice to come through the speaker.

A calm dispatcher answered, and I briefly shared what was happening. The first thing she said after asking for my most recent mile marker was, "Don't pull over!!!"

I chuckled under my breath at the absurd instruction. "I would never do that," I replied.

By this time, Julia was paying attention and had looked out the window. Thankfully, at her angle in the van, she could not see anything. However, she began to feel alarmed and anxious while listening to my conversation with the dispatcher and tried to ask what was going on. I couldn't fully respond but said, "Just wait!" I was trying to get the license plate number on his back bumper for the dispatcher. Any time I would speed up or slow down to read it, the man would do the same.

Does he know I'm trying to read his license plate? I wondered. However, *it seemed like it was just part of a routine he was used to doing.* I wanted to gag just from the thought of his potential intentions.

Soon, the 2-lane road turned into one, and he ensured I drove faster than him to follow me and avoid me reading his license plate. Finally, a gravel road appeared, which he took. *Thank God!* The dispatcher kept asking me more questions after he turned off and offered another obvious remark: "Don't follow him." *Are you kidding? This is the end of my Sherlock Holmes adventure for the day! I want to get as far away from this creep as possible.*

After the call ended, I realized how nervous I really was since I was shaking. I took some deep breaths to calm down and gave Julia a brief explanation. She settled down as well.

However, the trip from hell wasn't over.

We eventually stopped in Tupelo, Mississippi, at a gas station to fill up the van and go to the bathroom. I must have still been a bit befuddled from the event because after we got back to our vehicle, I realized the keys were inside it and the doors were locked.

Well, shit.

It was almost laughable as I was known for doing this, but that also meant I had AAA. The nice cashier inside allowed me to use their phone to make the call. The AAA representative said it would be about 45 minutes until they reached us, so we made it snack time as we waited. And waited. And waited.

After giving them a generous hour, I called again. They said it could be another 45 minutes! *Oh geez. We're never going to get to the clinic.* Then, attempting some positivity, I thought, *At least Denise and John didn't come with us this time.*

Another 45 minutes passed and still no one came. I spent the time trying to appease Julia, who had been restless and was unhappy, especially since her tailbone hurt from the hard seat. I called AAA again. They said it would be 20 minutes. This time, they were right. Twenty minutes later, help arrived in a red Datsun-like truck. Small trucks seemed to be haunting me that day.

Although the truck felt a bit deja vu, the people who were in it were quite a surprise. It was a whole family: a husband, wife, two children with tousled hair, bare feet, and who looked like they had rolled around in some mud and hadn't been bathed in a week, along with a pit bull mix on the bed of the truck. The husband looked like he had just woken up from a drunken sleep — could have been the reason for the long wait time — and came out to get my information.

Despite being a little concerned about who AAA had contracted for the job, I was breathing a sigh of relief. *We will be leaving soon.* Because of my previous experiences locking my keys inside vehicles, I knew they always had this quick tool they used to unlock them.

But nope, not today! The man went back to his truck and pulled out a WIRE CLOTHES HANGER! My confidence deflated, and some tears came to my eyes as the pit bull started to bark. (It seemed even the dog knew that the wire hanger wasn't going to work.) I asked the man if he had other tools, and he ignored me, but after several attempts, he couldn't get the vehicle open.

Soon the wife saw that he was struggling and exited the truck to help. She was wearing a house dress, house shoes, and curlers in her hair.

All the while their dog continued barking on and off, giving his moral support. This stressed me out because animals are usually fearful of Julia's wheelchair. Plus, although it was in the back of their truck, it wasn't on a leash. The couple yelled at it to "shut up" over and over as they tinkered with the door.

After an hour or so, they finally did it. The door was unlocked — and slightly warped for the rest of its life — the dog quieted, and we were on our way ... three hours behind schedule. But I knew the rest of the commute would be smooth sailing.

Or would it?

As we drove further south on a two-lane highway in the dim evening light, I noticed *another* old rusty antique truck loaded with rickety junk on a side road up ahead. "No, don't pull out, stay there, don't pull out!" I repeated.

Yep, it did! Right in front of me.

Blue smoke was billowing out of the muffler — the exhaust came through our vents — and there were no rear brake lights. I slowed way down to 30 mph and waited for the truck to speed up. But it never did. And it never left the highway we were driving.

I had always heard events arrive in threes.

Well, this is just terrific! Really, God? You have got to be kidding me! I muttered a few choice words and heard Julia say, "It's okay, Mom," trying to calm me more than once.

It didn't feel okay. I was so exhausted. And I wondered if it all was a sign. *Is He simply slowing me down or is He telling me I am not supposed to be at the clinic early this time to save me from something else for whatever reason? OR maybe He is telling me we shouldn't go to the clinic anymore? Are my dreams for Julia fading?* No answer.

With all of my doubts that had surfaced about Julia's treatment recently, I mulled over the latter question throughout the rest of the drive while tensely paying attention to the no-brake-lights truck, my hands tightly gripping the steering wheel, especially now that it was pitch-black. And when we finally arrived at the clinic, I helped Julia to bed and then, eventually, my brain turned off as I drifted to sleep.

"Blessed is the one who perseveres under trial because, having stood the test, that person will receive the crown of life that the Lord has promised to those who love him." (James 1:12)

Chapter 18

Julia was going to be attending first grade at the public school in the fall of 1998. After some years of homeschooling, the decision to send her to public school wasn't easy, but since Julia's physical progress was slowing, I figured she might as well go because it would benefit her to socialize with others. I knew even the smallest improvements could help prepare her for this life change and recalled an alternative treatment another parent had shared with me while at Futures Unlimited: the Tomatis method.

It was normal for me to research other therapies. In fact, over the years I had learned about live stem cell treatments in Germany (it seemed too expensive and far away); hyperbaric oxygen therapy (Julia's scar tissue on her lungs disqualified her); Botox for cerebral palsy patients to block the nerves that tell the spastic muscles to contract (we were wary of the toxicity); and Rhizotomy surgery during which the nerves are clipped, using chemical ablation or radio frequency ablation, along the spine to stop the message to the specific spastic muscles (I felt this was way to intrusive and the risks were too great). The Tomatis Method had been shared with me years before as well, but it hadn't been the time to delve into it. Now it was.

Marketed mostly for ADD/ADHD children, the Tomatis Method was a sound and light therapy. The center I had heard about previously, the Centre for Inner Change started by the late Dr. Ron Minson, used filtered Mozart music. When I called, the staff said the treatment was not cortical but that Julia would be listening to the music or looking at light therapy while wearing goggles and playing. Usually in a dimmed room.

They said it really helped some children and also did nothing for others. But for those it helped, the therapy had improved the children's attention spans, physical abilities, talking abilities, fine motor skills, muscle sensations with less reflective movements, and low muscle tone. One mom called me after her son had completed five days at the company's center in Maryland. She said he was already able to verbalize more and that his balance was better, though he still needed support. His moods had also improved.

From Ed's perspective, the Tomatis Method at the center was all cortical. He also felt it didn't have a developmental order, so he suggested not to try it. But I disagreed. I thought the treatment might enhance the CCDT results and was hoping these different sensory avenues could work together to make an even bigger difference for Julia.

The brochure stated that Mozart played his music in part for self-healing. I thought, *Perhaps it can still help heal people today in various ways.*

So I booked Julia's first appointment.

Third Alternative Treatment: Tomatis Method

Julia, Emily, my mom and I left for Denver in June. On the first day at the center, Julia went through some hearing assessments to see what tones she could or couldn't hear. This would direct them to formulate, or orchestrate, which Mozart tones to provide her.

After that, she listened.

To this day, I still don't know what filtered Mozart songs specifically Julia listened to for healing, but the one time I was able to experience light therapy, it was emotionally stirring and exhausting, so I can imagine what it was like. And I did see its effects in Julia afterward too.

Before the treatment, Julia still used her left hand to write. This was mostly due to the fact that her back strength and balance was better but would still give out or sway to the right some, leaving her left arm free. But just five days into the therapy, she automatically picked up her pencil to write with her right hand. I was so excited!

Ed had mentioned to me months before that if we sent Julia to school, we should NOT allow the teachers to force her to write with her left hand. He had performed a few physical genetic tests and said she was hereditarily right-handed. So, if they forced her to write with her left hand, she could become dyslexic, which seemed to be correct because when Julia chose her left hand to write, she always started on the right side of the paper and wrote in a mirror image. When she used her right hand to write, she would start on the left side of the paper and the letters were written correctly.

Julia now having the ability to do more with her dominant hand was a huge win in my eyes, even a miracle! I later told Kathy with conviction that God really had *His* hand guiding my decision to take her to Denver to experience this new treatment.

While we were at the center, Dr. Minson also recommended that Julia make an appointment with a nutritionist, so we did. The nutritionist asked us to get a stool sample to send to the lab, and we found out a week or so after we returned home that the lab results noted she had a LOT of parasites.

At home, Julia would crawl to the fridge to eat bread with ketchup on top and drink pickle juice. I didn't think it was odd because all three of those items are what we ate with our meals, but the nutritionist said it was a clear indication.

"When someone feels like they constantly need foods like bread with ketchup, pickle juice, and a lot of sugar, it is a sure sign that there is an imbalance, and parasites will feast and multiply," she explained.

I had no idea!

We returned home with a strict low-carb diet, nothing aged, no condiments, low dairy, no alcohol, nothing fried, and nothing white. JUST meat, vegetables, and limited fruit. That meant no pizza, no fried chicken, no potatoes, no biscuits and gravy, etc. Well, you get the idea! All our favorite food for the most part had to disappear. The nutritionist also recommended specific herbs for her to eliminate the parasites.

This diet was going to be very difficult. I could not see how it would work to cook for Julia alone *and* cook a regular meal for the rest of us, so I started all four of us on this diet. My husband and Emily got tired of it really quickly. I was disappointed but understood. It was not easy. So, I decided to go on the diet with Julia and just added a little something for the other two to eat in addition to what we ate. This way at least Julia did not have to do it by herself.

We were on this diet for three months. It felt like an eternity, but we did it! Well, for the most part. Julia shared with me later that she cheated. While I was busy one day, she crawled to the fridge and made another ketchup sandwich. A few hours later, I asked, "Who left the crumbs on the floor by the fridge?"

Julia had a beautiful complexion after going on the diet, and the dark circles under her eyes had almost disappeared. Most importantly, her stools became more bearable. And in six weeks, I lost 15 lbs. Although I was not overweight, the fewer pounds made me feel even healthier. So, it was a win for both of us.

We booked another trip to the Centre for Inner Change the following year, but we didn't see any improvements after that trip. I figured Julia attained what she was going to, so we never returned. But what she had accomplished was monumental and another miracle. She would go to school writing with her right hand!

It changes direction, turning around by His guidance, That it may do whatever He commands it On the face of the inhabited earth. (Job 37:12)

Let's hold firmly to the confession of our hope without wavering, for He who promised is faithful. (Hebrews 10:23)

PART 3

CHAPTER 19

JULIA ATTENDED LAWSON ELEMENTARY at 8 years old as a first grader. It was the first time she had been in a classroom, and she did well!

Initially, she didn't want to go. However, she *did* want to do all the same things as her big sister, which helped overcome her reluctance. Plus, I got her excited about riding the bus.

I followed it the first morning to put me at ease, but to be completely honest, my heart was heavier than I expected. I had always pictured Julia walking onto the bus on her first day of school.

I fully appreciated how big this moment was for her; we had taken first day of school pictures just like we had done with Emily. But the joy didn't arrive without grief, and that day, the heartache had the louder voice, even as her sweet smiling face looked at me through the bus window.

From then on, Julia always rode the bus by herself, unloaded with the lift, and rolled into the special needs room where Susie, the special needs coordinator, greeted her. Susie was very supportive and seemed to take a special interest in Julia, and Julia delighted in wrapping people around her little finger. However, Susie and her team always ensured Julia's wheelchair seat belt was fastened. Julia was showing some rebellion at that point in her life and didn't like the seatbelt fastened, so she would take it off outside of Susie's room and fasten it again before she returned to her room.

Susie found out and was even more resolved that she wear it, which meant Julia did NOT want to go to school anymore. But we talked about it, why it was important to avoid accidents, why Susie was so persistent that she had it buckled because she had her best interest at heart, and that it was her job to keep Julia safe. Julia relented and said she would go back to school. Eventually, the two of them grew to have a very special bond.

When Julia got to second grade, Lawson Elementary received a grant that provided the school with partitioned wooden tables with shelving on top of them. They were placed for four students, and to me, they looked like cubicles, a divide of sorts for the students.

"Why would they do this!" I wondered aloud to my sister. "Is it a psychological experiment?

Needless to say, my husband and I decided to send Julia to the same school as Emily, St. Martin's Elementary, so Julia would avoid this type of classroom. Although there was some hesitancy from the staff at first, they were very accommodating and inviting. Her teacher, Ms. Rachel Swillum, was beyond accepting of her and could tell she was a "very determined young lady." It wasn't hard for adults to like Julia. She was such a happy child most of the time and exuded fun. She once typed "I like myself" in computer class. Julia drew people to her — and we were in her shadow. I was grateful for this because I didn't want her to be dismissed due to her disability.

Julia made some friends at St. Martin's too. One of them was a sweet little boy who would push her around during recess. It was always done respectfully, but after a while, Julia asked that he wouldn't push her anymore because she liked being in control of her chair. He agreed, and she was glad to have him as her friend still. I was happy because she was starting to show her independence.

This year went as smoothly as any school year could go. I was checking in on Julia regularly and many days even helping Ms. Swillum in her classroom.

The girls enjoy school for the most part, but some early mornings were difficult. I would wake up and start breakfast after going to each of their bedrooms and telling them it was time to get up. After a little while, I couldn't hear any movement, so I'd go back, turn on their lights, and remind them to get out of bed. Minutes later, there was still nothing.

So finally, I would go back to their bedrooms again and begin loudly clapping and dancing while singing: *"Rise and shine, and give God the glory, glory! Rise and shine, and give God the glory, glory! Rise and shine and give God the glory, glory, children of the Lord!!"*

Needless to say, grunts and groans would arise from the bed. Emily would quickly slap the covers over her head while moaning, "MOOOOM!" Julia yelled, "STOOOOP!" And after a couple repetitions of the verse, they begrudgingly got up to eat breakfast before heading out the door.

By the end of the year, Susie from Lawson Elementary called and asked how Julia was doing. She said the school had gotten rid of the partitioned tables and asked if Julia would be coming back. We talked to Julia, and she agreed to return. Even though her experience at St. Martin's was good, she would be given more services at the public school.

However, this didn't mean the public school was finally willing to include Julia's CCDT treatment services. After another IEP meeting, I realized that it would be impossible to change the district's policies. So, I did it with her at home as much as we were able. We also continued to go to Futures Unlimited for reduced 10-day sessions a couple times each year. Julia would miss school, but the teachers sent her work with us so she wouldn't get behind. Emily decided to stay home at this point and spent time with her cousins and friends.

Yes, our busy routine was still in full swing, even with Julia having gone to school for the past two years. And yet, everything was different. Although I missed seeing my girls like I had been while homeschooling, it was also nice to have more time to myself during the day. And I had been using quite a bit of that time to design and oversee the building of our new home, which would accommodate Julia's accessibility needs.

It was the most fun I had experienced on my own in a long time! I had always loved designing houses. I remember as a child, around 12 years old, sitting in my dad's recliner with Mom's dining table leaf in front of me resting on the recliner arms. It was there that I would use a piece of grid paper and become absorbed in creating my dream homes. Although I was now an adult, I felt like that kid again. I drew and erased, drew and erased and drew some more into the wee hours of the morning until I knew I had to get some sleep.

And what resulted from my designs was a one-level ranch-style home with wide hallways and doors, complete with a treatment room and a great room for ease of movement and family gatherings. I love windows, so the main space had a bank of them. There were also some large ones over the kitchen sink, which faced East so the sunrise could flood the kitchen. A sunroom overlooked our green backyard where some very old sycamore trees were still growing. Past that, I was so detailed that I even planned out what would be stored in each of the drawers in my favorite room, the kitchen.

The home turned out beautifully, and we moved into it in 1999. It was a dream come true for all of us. Yet there were still more dreams to be realized.

"May the favor of the Lord our God rest on us; establish the work of our hands for us — yes, establish the work of our hands." (Psalm 90:17)

CHAPTER 20

OUR LIFE NEEDED SOME normalcy, meaning we needed to do something other than therapy. So, we decided to treat the girls to Walt Disney World and Universal Studios. This was my chance to get us together as a family and go on a real vacation, no therapy involved.

We told the girls we were going to Disney World ... the night before! They were beyond excited, and Emily barely slept. It would be their first time at a theme park and also their first time on an airplane. They didn't care for the flight very much but were proud to receive their wings from the airline attendant.

While the flight could have been more appealing to the girls, nothing could take away from the magic that Walt Disney World, specifically, held for them. We spent time at all four theme parks (Magic Kingdom, Animal Kingdom, Hollywood Studios, and EPCOT), plus Disney's Blizzard Beach Water Park. They were long days that created tired feet and often felt overwhelming because of the crowds being shoulder to shoulder, but they were worth it!

Julia's favorite ride was the Toy Story one called Buzz Lightyear's Space Ranger Spin during which you shoot at bright targets while in the dark. She rode it multiple times with her dad because the staff let her stay on and ride it again instead of making her get off to get back in her wheelchair just to get back on the ride again. She was elated, and I think her dad had as much fun as she did!

Emily and I rode the wild indoor outer space-themed ride: Space Mountain. We squealed and screamed with a little fright as we wooshed by other riders. I glanced over at Emily as best as I could while being jerked around, and the smile on her face was all I needed to see. She was loving it! By the end, we couldn't keep away the exhilarated smiles and laughter as we exited the galaxy and found the sunshine again.

We also rode the The Twilight Zone Tower of Terror at Disney's Hollywood Studios. My husband and Julia thought we were crazy, but they waited for us as we walked into the haunted hotel and got into the elevator shaft where we experienced the sound of cracking cables and quick drops that caused my sunglasses hanging around my neck to float above my head. Although we decided not to get in line again, we had fun!

There was only one ride that didn't go so well for us all, but mostly for Julia. Splash Mountain was a water roller coaster, Br'er Rabbit-themed, and fairly calm … until you reached the end of the ride where there was what seemed like a 90-degree drop that went on for 50+ feet into gigantic "briars." Julia was in panic mode. I told her to hang onto me while I held onto her, and when she did, it was a death grip.

We went down — Julia screaming at the top of her lungs. And what I thought would be a fun experience turned out to be a memorable experience but not in a good way. When we had made it to the bottom, we were windblown, and Julia was terror-stricken. She said she would never ride a roller coaster again.

Thank goodness there were other good highlights during the trip. We took a scheduled bus to our breakfast with Tigger and Pooh, and the girls loved meeting Tigger! We were also mesmerized by the fireworks that lit up the sky every night.

We returned home with great memories and a little more pep in our steps. Disney World may not really be the "happiest place on earth" — home is the best! — but it sure feels like it when you're there.

The next time we went on vacation, which was a few years later, it was to Colorado. Amy, Jerry and their family were going to Winter Park to ski and invited us and my mother-in-law to go with them. How exciting! But also a little nerve-wracking as my family had never skied before.

I always told my girls that they could do anything, and this was one way to prove it. So I researched how it would be possible for Julia and found that the AmeriCorps provided skiing services to the disabled at Winter Park. On our first day, after Julia was fitted for the sit ski and received a tutorial, I waved goodbye to her as she left with the AmeriCorps volunteers for the ski lift.

I will admit that it felt very odd seeing my disabled daughter get on a ski lift with strangers! But I watched a little longer, reminded myself that they do it all the time, and knew she would be fine. Then the rest of us went to the bunny slope for orientation.

Emily and I got the hang of it fairly easily, and we all were on the green slopes by lunch. It was almost as much fun riding the ski lift, where I could take in the cool crisp air, beautiful sunshine, few clouds, and gorgeous mountain scenery, as it was to ski.

Julia would typically get cold very easily, so she couldn't sit-ski all day, but she really enjoyed the experience. A bungee cord was attached to the back and front of her sit-ski sled with an AmeriCorps volunteer connected to the bungee cords. This balanced her and taught her to use the outriggers to balance herself. By the third day, she was told she could start sit-skiing independently. She attempted it, but didn't ski that way for long. She preferred letting the others do the work for her because it was much more fun. So she was more sledding than sit-skiing, but she tried!

On the last day, it had snowed overnight, which left light loose snow, so it was difficult to ski. Julia didn't go that morning, and I fell and twisted my knee. Thankfully it was minor, but it ended the day prematurely. Nonetheless, I was thankful for the trip, especially to Amy's family for sharing the experience with us, and I was proud of everyone in our family for being courageous.

In 2002, another exciting travel opportunity presented itself. Every three years, the local Girl Scouts council planned an international trip. The next one was in 2003 to Hawaii, Australia, and New Zealand, and Emily and I discovered that a local Girl Scout group was planning to go. Amy and my niece, Christy, were also interested, so we called the other Girl Scouts troop leader to see if we could join in. They said no. But that didn't stop us! Amy and I decided to start a troop just for Emily and Christy and began fundraising. We had one year to raise the money.

Christy, Emily and I went blackberry picking in the summer and sold the berries we picked. We had three garage sales and cleaned houses. Emily even applied for one of the Girl Scouts scholarships and received some money from that. But we were nearing the spring and both girls were still coming up a little short.

So we planned a big event!

At about 3:30 a.m. on a dark Sunday morning, we left for St. Louis — Amy and Christy in their SUV, and Emily and me in our van — to pick up 450 dozen Krispy Kreme donuts. Krispy Kreme was the rave back then, and people had been partnering with it for fundraisers, but Jefferson City didn't have a store, hence the trip to St. Louis. It took two hours to get there, and then we had to drive home, the boxes crammed in the now sweet donut-smelling van and Amy's SUV.

Once we got back, we set up shop on the busy Missouri Boulevard. For hours, we waved our arms, smiled, and yelled out "Krispy Kreme Donuts!" We were so thankful when people stopped.

It was hot, we didn't have enough water or food to eat all day (we snuck a few doughnuts but didn't want to eat all our profit), but we stuck it out until late afternoon approached. With sunburned faces, we left there and set up near a local gas station before heading to our church to sell them after Mass ended because we still had about 40 dozen left. A few more dozen were sold. The next morning, we set up after 10 a.m. Mass and only had 10 dozen left.

There was no plan B if we didn't sell them, and thankfully we didn't need one. The rest were shared with family and friends until they were gone. It was a long day and a half, and we were exhausted. But it felt like we had raked in a fortune while counting and dividing the money between us, and ... it was enough.

We would be going abroad!

The international tour was amazing, and I loved sharing it with Emily. In Hawaii, a 36-hour stop, we saw the USS Arizona, enjoyed a luau, and snorkeled. In New Zealand, we rode one of the steepest cogwheel railways in the world, saw a sheep shearing demonstration, visited the area where *The Lord of the Rings* was filmed, watched the traditional Māori haka dance, and viewed and smelled the geothermal bubbling sulfur mud ponds in Rotorua. We were awestruck by the beautiful landscape on our way to Auckland.

From there, we flew to Sydney, Australia. We went on a tour of and saw a symphony at the Sydney Opera House and found a city under the city. I didn't even know something like this existed! We rode the steepest passenger railway to see the Three Sisters rock formations in the rainforest of the Blue Mountains. Our very long flight back had a 12-hour layover in Santa Monica, so we took a city bus to the beach for some rest. I told Amy while she drove us home that I felt like I was still flying.

We were so blessed. Trips like this made me feel like I was finally being rewarded for all my previous years traveling for therapy and doing therapy, which never lended much free time, and for all the years of those same routines that were to come.

"For I know the plans I have for you," declares the Lord, "plans to prosper you not to harm you, plans to give you hope and a future." (Jeremiah 29:11)

CHAPTER 21

By this time, Julia was growing up into adolescence, and she was experiencing some symptoms. She wanted to stay home from middle school and didn't want to be around a lot of people, which was abnormal because she seemed to flourish when with them.

She also didn't want to eat and was losing weight. Julia was already thin from cerebral palsy, but it was more than that, though I was in denial and did not believe it was anything serious. I didn't understand and decided that it was just a phase, that she was likely looking for attention and she would grow out of it. Sometimes she would be herself, but other times not.

I'm sure it didn't help that Julia had recently fractured her right tibia. I had been out of town with Emily at one of her cheer competitions, and when we arrived home that Sunday, I noticed Julia couldn't put any weight on her right leg while transferring. And when she tried to, tears filled her eyes.

I asked her what happened, and she said she fell off the four-wheeler and had twisted her leg. So Monday morning, I took her to the doctor.

They asked me to leave the room so they could talk to Julia by herself. Although I understood this to be protocol, it was a little upsetting that someone thought

I would *ever* hurt my daughter. I was also upset that I hadn't been home when it happened. Yes, it was an accident, but she hadn't been taken to any medical facility immediately; instead, there had been a standstill until I returned. And thank goodness I took her in because the doctors told me she had a spiral fracture.

Waiting on her leg to heal had only worsened Julia's depressed demeanor. She said it was the longest eight weeks of her life. She couldn't do much for herself outside of keeping mobile with her chair, so she had to be lifted up to the kitchen counter to wash her hair at the sink, and when she did take a sponge bath, her cast had to be covered in plastic so it wouldn't get wet. But even after her leg had healed, she continued to struggle as if the cast was still there.

One day around age 13, she was sitting in the living room chair and hadn't eaten much for about three days. Her eyes were sunken in and just staring out, eerily watching me.

Finally, her dad and I asked her blankly if she wanted to die.

Silence.

Feeling defeated, I walked away, through the hallway, and toward the back of the house, but after some seconds had passed, my spirit turned my body around. I was mad. Not at her, but at the situation. Yet I marched unwaveringly back into the room and yelled at her. "I have a child with cerebral palsy! By damn, I'm not having a child with anorexia too!"

Julia then cried and cried and said she didn't want to die. I walked up and hugged her, while her dad responded earnestly, "Then EAT!"

After that, she started eating slowly. She seemed to have fewer episodes, but they came in waves. None of it seemed to make sense, and she couldn't determine why she felt the way she did. We were working with Dr. Shipman, our naturopathic doctor, who continued to pray over Julia and offer support by balancing her systems with herbs and vitamins. This seemed to make everything more manageable, but even that wasn't a complete fix.

Perhaps Julia was noticing more and more how different she was because she was the only person in her class and in middle school who used a wheelchair. She also had tonal outburst related to cerebral palsy when she was nervous or got excited at, say, a sporting event. The other students seemed to be kind, and one of her aides was an absolute blessing and did everything she could to understand what Julia was going through.

But even kindness couldn't always make it easier. Julia constantly carried an emotional weight. And this made me confused, frustrated, scared, so very tired, and, above all else, sad. Sad for Julia having to hit rough patch after rough patch in her already challenging life. I wanted life to give her a break.

"But now, Lord, what do I look for? My hope is in you." (Proverbs 39:7)

CHAPTER 22

WHEN EMILY STARTED HIGH school and Julia was in middle school, I decided it was time for a change. My girls were growing up, and while I was still very much "Mom," I wasn't needed all hours of the day anymore. Plus, their four high school-age cousins (Lindsey, Leslie, Courtney, and Christy) took turns helping with Julia's therapy too, so I felt I could work full time. They offered a break for me and Julia.

A second income would also be a great help to our family. I had quit Pampered Chef a few years before and knew I didn't want to return to retail if I didn't have to, so I began to dream again about what a new field like architecture/drafting, real estate sales, insurance sales and massage therapy would look like. However, annual leave and benefits sure sparked my interest as well, and after researching state jobs, I applied and accepted a position with the Missouri Department of Industrial Relations. It sounded as boring as it was, though I was grateful for the job.

One downside to it was that this position paid less than what I received when I resigned from my career job twelve years before. I anticipated starting with less pay, however, it was still disappointing.

On top of that, I had a very limiting boss, to say the least. She watched everything I did, and there were no gray areas. If I came back from lunch 15 minutes late because I needed to run some errands and they took longer, I couldn't tag on those 15 minutes to the end of the day to get my hours worked. Instead, she told me I could take annual leave for the time missed. But my annual leave was always used for helping Julia, taking her to doctor's appointments, or dealing with any emergencies. The job made me feel suffocated, and I found myself checking the time wondering when the next break would be or if it was time to go home. So I quickly began looking online for state positions in other departments.

One came through for me in the Grants Management Section in the Division of State Parks. While I was hoping for a full-time position, I was informed that it was part time. Initially I was disappointed but soon realized what a gift it was. I could make money to help provide for our family and still take Julia out of state to her clinic sessions. But even more exciting, it would also allow me the time to go back to school to learn more about massage therapy.

Many years ago, after graduating high school, I had seriously thought about three different careers: fashion merchandising, cosmetology, and massage therapy. Fashion merchandising won over cosmetology, and my protective, yet loving, mom gave me too many reasons why I shouldn't go into the massage profession. The reasons were mostly related to male clients. "You're a pretty girl," she said. "You never know what will happen in a room with a man by yourself." I understood her concern but always thought I could have handled it, though I did relent and allowed her to talk me out of pursuing it as a career.

That desire to do massage therapy never went away. When I received my first massage while working at JCPenney, I said enthusiastically to the therapist, "Where has this been all my life!" And after coming full circle and spending years doing Julia's massages, my passion had only grown. Mostly I wanted to know more about how to help Julia, but if I could possibly help other people too, that would be awesome! I decided it was my time. I applied to attend the Massage Therapy Institute of Missouri in Columbia, Missouri, and started classes in January 2005.

The school was enlightening, and I loved learning about all the facets of the body and different modalities that are offered. One of my teachers was a craniosacral therapist, or CST, so we were introduced to this type of therapy over the course of her class. It is totally different from CCDT and uses a gentle, hands-on technique to release the tension around the body's fascia, or the connective tissue surrounding the muscles, organs, nerves, etc.

I wondered if it would help Julia. She had been dealing with chronic headaches, and craniosacral therapy was supposed to target them. So, not too long after I passed the grueling national massage therapist exam (yay!), I made plans to take Julia to Florida where she would receive her first treatment in the summer of 2006.

Fourth Alternative Treatment: Craniosacral Therapy

It was a weeklong session. Julia received treatment for a couple hours in the mornings on therapy tables with up to three therapists at a time (though it was usually one or two). I would bring her lunch, and we'd eat on a patio before she underwent two or more hours of therapy in the afternoon. The rest of the day was free time.

Julia liked the treatment and how it made her feel. Her face looked more rounded and relaxed, she could sit up straighter and was more at ease, and she said her headaches had lessened. "It's like my head is now screwed on right," she explained.

We would be back.

And I decided that, upon returning home, I would use the gentle CST techniques during my massage sessions with clients. After graduating massage school, I contacted the local hospital, which offered me a small room for massage in a quiet hallway. The hospital only charged me a minimal amount per massage to rent it, and I could use the hospital sheets. The staff would also pick up the dirty laundry and return clean ones to me the next day. It was perfect!

At the time, the going rate for massage therapy was about $55-60. I charged $50 since I was just starting out but was hoping to increase my fee after I had more continuing education hours and took on more and more clients. I was also hoping to do massage full time and quit my part-time job with the Division of State Parks. But it didn't happen.

It was difficult to obtain referrals, and I didn't market myself well, plus I was still juggling the part-time job *and* Julia's therapy. Running a business was more difficult than I anticipated. Per usual, I was also impatient and wanted more income faster. I was notified that the person at State Parks was retiring and I could possibly increase to full time with benefits again, so after just a couple years doing massage on the side, I stopped and pursued this option.

But I hadn't given up hope and the spark was still there for my massage therapy business. I continued to give massages to Julia and a handful of others, and I reminded myself that I had put this passion off (as well as others) before.

I could wait a little longer.

———— *ele* ————

"I wait for the LORD, my soul waits, and in his word I hope."

(Psalms 130:5)

"If God is for us, who can be against us?"

(Romans 9:31)

Chapter 23

We had been slowly decreasing our visits to Futures Unlimited. This allowed us to try other modalities, but also, Ed, the remarkable man, but who was getting older and facing some of his own health issues. In August 2006, I received a call from Susan, his daughter, informing us with a heaviness that he was in the hospital with pneumonia and was not doing well.

I had known Ed for 14 years, and we had developed a close friendship. Julia couldn't even remember her life before him. When I heard the news, there was no hesitation. I knew we needed to see him — one last time. This man had poured so much of himself into Julia's progress. And more than that, we wanted to say goodbye.

We arrived at the hospital in Mississippi and found his room. I noticed Julia pulling back and didn't want to go in, which was surprising, but I allowed her to process what was happening however she needed to and went in by myself. I was also hesitant, because I wasn't sure what I would see, but there he was asleep, frail, but still the same man I had come to love. He definitely looked ill and older from what his body had been put through.

I turned to the nurse with a wondering look on my face, and she nodded to go ahead. I whispered his name as I walked up by the bed and touched his arm. He groggily opened his eyes, and then a smile rose to his cheeks with the same kind eyes I remembered. I couldn't help but smile back at him.

We talked for a little while. I told him he didn't belong in a hospital room like this and that I was praying he would recover and get back to his home. "You'll be better in no time," I said, which wasn't just a reassuring comment to him but also for me. With tears in my eyes, I thanked him for everything he had done for Julia and my family over the years — his hope in her potential when others saw limitations. And I told him he had become a part of our family and that I loved him.

There was a grumble in his lungs, and he started to cough. I placed my hand on his chest/heart, and we were quiet for a short while. The noise from his lungs ceased.

"You have a healing touch," he told me. "My coughing stopped." Then, he added, "You have a gift. Never stop sharing it."

I promised him I wouldn't.

Julia came in a few minutes later, and the reunion was a happy one. We didn't stay too long for fear of tiring Ed out, but before we left, he did request that we only do his treatment in the future. And I agreed. Deep down, though, I knew I couldn't follow through with this promise because no one else was performing CCDT, I had already tried a couple other types of therapy, and I knew I would continue to search for other ways to heal Julia. So it must have been a weak moment — a desire to please a man who was going to see the Lord.

And he did see Him. Edward A. "Ed" Snapp passed away on August 16, 2006, at his home. He was a one-of-a-kind human being. Not only had he developed his therapy for central nervous system injuries to help others, including my daughter, but he also treated his patients like family. Julia and I had made many trips to

Futures Unlimited, and every time we went to the clinic or called to ask him for advice, we felt his love and care. I loved Ed like a brother and looked up to him like a father. There would never be another like him. Even his company's name exuded hope.

In light of Ed's passing, his son, James, wrote a touching eulogy about him that encapsulated his heart for others.

MORE THAN ADJUSTMENTS & ASSESSMENTS

Ed Snapp was an incredible thinker and, in my opinion, one of the nicest men that ever lived. His ability to think in retrospect gave him the vision of seeing how human functions developed and how to find the foundational deficit related to various disabilities. This unique ability allowed him the insight to group not just one or two diagnoses together but an entire array of neurological and developmental disabilities. In a thought, it seems that we will one day see that if a functional disability is not related to extreme nervous tissue damage, then it should be repairable strictly by neuro-sensory sequencing. Because of Ed Snapp's work, medical professionals will someday see that properly organized basic sensations are remarkably responsible for the recovery of core functional aspects of our bodies and central nervous systems.

Besides the fact that Edward A Snapp Jr. was my father, it is safe for me to say that his life was an awe-inspiring gift for anyone who had been in the room with him. He never expected anything from anyone, and he always gave them everything he had in him. People were always given hope because his heart only knew how to help.

There is a way to help, even if it is just by giving a glimmer of hope. Do you believe that? I do. I have to because that is how I was raised. Even when you are down and out, there is still a chance you will get back to where you can rise up again. Never give up completely, not until the very end. You know, Ed Snapp was that kind of man. That is the kind of therapy that a man like that produces. One that gives hope. One that doesn't say, "We're done here."

The truth is that there is hope for many people struggling with disabilities, trauma, dysfunction, learning problems, autism, brain injury, you name it. The best part is that, as a nation and a world, we are beginning to see the wonder of what God has given us. Natural medicine. It has been here since the beginning. Our best doctor is right within our very cells. What a time of life to be here on earth and what a wonder to uplift so many people.

Thank you, Ed Snapp, for what you have done. You are loved always! Your steady and selfless ways have done so much for so many. I know that your dreams of natural recovery from spinal injury, brain injuries, and other traumatic injuries will come true. I know that your amazing display of care for others will not go unappreciated in this world. I know that because of your amazing will to help those who want to believe in hope, that in the present time, many have a chance to live to their fullest again. Ed always said, "Son, do your best." Truly I don't know if I've lived up to that, but I know I sure am willing. There are not many in this world who focus on others' benefit. There are not many in this world who truly care how you are. Don't we need to strengthen one another? Isn't that how we do our best? It is a tough life, and this world is a hard place to live, but if there is one thing we need, it is to do our best to care about one another. That is the mission of this life. Let's do our best to love one another. Ed did his part, now let's do ours.

James E Snapp CMT, LMT ~ The hopeful son of a great and awesome man.

Ed once asked me early on in our friendship if I thought I could be an astronaut. "Probably not, but I hope I can." Then I added with a laugh, "Even though I don't have a desire to do that!"

"Well," he replied with sincerity, "Just remember, you can do whatever you set your mind to do."

He was a true blessing. Ed had always given me hope to look for more for my daughters and myself in every aspect of life. He taught me to never give up, and I didn't. I still don't. Because there is always hope for another glimmer of a small miracle.

"Sustain me according to Your word, that I may live; And do not let me be ashamed of my hope."

(Psalms 119:6)

"And hope does not put us to shame, because God's love has been poured out into our hearts through the Holy Spirit, who has been given to us."

(Romans 5:5)

CHAPTER 24

I CAN'T SAY HIGH school was the time in which we saw many of those miracles. I don't think most parents would say the teenage years were the best years, but for the most part, all of us (me included) made it through them okay.

Emily and Julia each had their own experience. Emily attended Helias High School, a private Catholic school (the same one I went to when I was young). When she attended St. Martins, she was involved in softball, volleyball, and her eighth grade year she liked competitive cheer. But it cost the same per year to be on the cheer team as it did per year to attend Helias, so I gave Emily the choice: go to public school and cheer or go to private school. She chose Helias.

Emily enjoyed the private school even though, in general, she didn't care for school. She made friends there, dated some, and stayed busy. We didn't see her as much because she kept to herself; I wondered if she was simply finding her own way. But she was very involved in community plays and musicals, and I loved watching her perform.

The productions varied every year and included: *Nottingham: A Totally Teen Musical*; *Jason and the Argonauts*; *The Lion, The Witch, and The Wardrobe*; *Chicago*; *West Side Story*; *High School Musical* and more. Emily was typically a side character but soon grew to play more prominent parts. Our favorite was her role as Janey in *The Merry Go Round*. Emily had to act out her character as a 7–year-old, 20-year-old, 40-year-old, and *very* old lady. She NAILED the old lady's voice, which she created at dress rehearsal!

Sophomore year she also joined Young Life, a nondenominational christian ministry that provided weekly services for high schoolers. I picked her up one evening from a service and, having arrived early, I rolled down my window to hear the music. The praise and worship had a contemporary sound, which included a rock beat. I enjoyed listening to it, but it was very different from the music they played at my Catholic church, which had a more reverent sound with fewer instruments accompanying the singing. Emily also invited me to go to a Baptist church service, and while there I felt a stirring I couldn't explain. She nudged me and said, "Mom, that's the Holy Spirit!"

I wasn't upset that Emily was going to Young Life meetings — if it was leading her to Christ, then why not? — but I did wonder why she wasn't finding fulfillment in the Catholic faith. And it concerned me a little that she was looking for more answers outside of what Catholicism taught, which is the only type of religion I knew and what I preferred for her.

But in a way, I also understood her shift. Once I was crying in the cry room at my church during Mass because the priest had said something like "anything that happens to us is our fault." This wasn't too long after we received Julia's diagnosis and I thought, *What!? How could my innocent child being given this situation be her fault?*

I went home feeling the sting of the priest's words and chose not to attend church regularly again until the priest was commissioned elsewhere. I didn't believe what was said, but I definitely couldn't call out and argue against it because I didn't know the Bible well enough to back my stance. Through Young Life, though, I watched Emily take a deeper dive into the Bible, so much so that her Bible was beginning to look a little worn. She knew more about what was in those pages than I did.

When Emily became a senior, I told her that I'd like her to be confirmed in the Catholic faith. This is a Sacrament in the Catholic Church in which the one who is confirmed is strengthened by the Holy Spirit's gifts through the anointing of chrism and laying of hands. Emily didn't want to do it, but eventually begrudgingly agreed, which meant she had to attend a weekly class with other high school seniors for about six months.

During those classes, I learned that she corrected the teacher about what was in the Bible and what the scriptures meant. I was a little embarrassed for the teacher because it sounded like Emily came across as "I'm right" and "You are wrong," but it also seemed that she *was* right! She knew her Bible, and I couldn't blame her for wanting the truth to prevail.

Emily was also asked to give her testimony during a Young Life fundraiser benefit dinner and auction. She invited me to attend, and I wouldn't miss it! When we arrived, I was amazed. And concerned. I didn't know it was such a huge event with around 300 people in attendance, and Emily had told me that she didn't prepare anything.

But my precious child didn't seem nervous at all as she went up on stage, talked like she had prepared for hours, and gave a well-spoken, and longer than expected, testimony about her experience with Young Life and what it meant to her. Her years in theater seemed to have only elevated her speaking skills and confidence in front of a crowd, and my heart was full of pride and joy!

That's my baby!! I proclaimed internally.

Afterward, on the way home, I told her she was doing what was right for her and that I was happy she found something that gave her peace. In a way, her testimony had granted me the peace I needed to let go of our denomination differences too while she finished out her senior year.

When Julia got to high school, we found the hallways to be just as narrow as her middle school ones, and crowded. This made things difficult for her to get around. She would also leave a little early for the next class so she wasn't having to follow people very often. At one point, I asked her why she did it.

"Mom, think about it," she said jokingly. "What am I looking at all day in the hallways?!" I understood! It couldn't be fun consistently having to stare at people's butts. But we both couldn't help ourselves, and chuckled about this reality.

Julia's "episodes" also continued intermittently into high school. We weren't exactly sure what to call them because we weren't exactly sure what they were and why they were happening. No one else seemed to understand them either.

During the episodes, her body would become even stiffer than it usually was due to her cerebral palsy spasticity, and she would inconsistently have trouble swallowing, feel very fatigued and a little disoriented. Her hands would get sweaty, sometimes her heart would race, and there was some shortness of breath.

I blamed the occurrences on her not eating enough or drinking enough water. Or maybe she didn't get enough sleep, someone looked at her the wrong way, or was nervous because she had a test. It seemed I was using any excuse because … I wasn't sure. But Julia didn't know how to cope with them and often took out her frustration on our dog, Jodee, though Jodee didn't take it without giving a warning and a bite once.

There were a few bigger events at school too during which Julia was sent to the nurse's office and her blood pressure had gone up. They would give her a Dr.

Pepper thinking her blood sugar was low. The nurse also said she should go on some kind of medication. But we chose not to put her on any because it seemed like a temporary solution and her episodes were so few and sporadic.

Julia finished her freshman year at the public school, but because of the issues she had been facing there, I wondered if she would be better off at Helias where Emily was attending. During the previous two years, Helias had undertaken a huge renovation, which included a new gym, more classrooms, a larger cafeteria, and an elevator. This made the school accessible.

I talked to Julia, and she was willing to try switching schools, particularly because she thought it would be a calmer environment since it was Christian-based. So we asked Helias if they would accept Julia. Although they didn't have any handicapped students and the staff to help her with an IEP, I told them we could start with what we used from the public school system and that we would provide her aide ourselves. They agreed.

It was a bit of a culture shock for Julia at first, and her episodes still occurred from time to time too, but they had lessened, and there were some wonderful aspects of her attending Helias.

Overall the school had a community feel, it wasn't as loud, and there were fewer students, so they were able to focus on each student as an individual. Everyone was in a uniform. Her aide took notes for her so that she could keep up with the classwork. Tests were taken verbally because Julia couldn't write fast enough to get the test done in the class period. Another blessing.

The teachers there were wonderful, and per usual, Julia got along well with them. One in particular, Ms. Noonan, stood out among the rest. She not only taught Julia ... she *saw* her. She took time to connect with her after school. Ms. Noonan also asked if Julia would give her a quote of the day to put on the bulletin board for the following morning. Julia loved finding inspirational quotes for her classmates;

words about strength, hope, and kindness. She loved the idea of encouraging others, and it became one of her favorite parts of high school.

Julia loved frequenting the sports games (basketball, baseball, football, volleyball). She had watched her cousins' play over the years and now consistently supported her classmates at Helias. A few of the basketball guys would take turns and go to the conference room to eat lunch with her. The cafeteria was too stimulating — loud, crowded, brightly lit. The conference room was quiet, which put her at ease and allowed her to make friends with some of the basketball guys more easily.

Because Julia loved watching sports, we went once a year to see some other sports teams play too. One time we were at a Mizzou football game watching her cousin's boyfriend, Phil, play. I had to go to the bathroom and told her to sit tight. "I'll be back in three minutes."

As I began to stand up, I heard, "I have to go too!"

I hesitated, wondering if she really did need to or if she didn't want to be left by herself. I told her to talk to Nellie, a woman we always sat by at the games. "Yes, watch the game with me, Julia," Nellie encouraged.

However, Julia was adamant that she had to go, so I said, "Okay, let's hurry. Well, of course, there is no hurrying when it comes to Julia. However, we were leaving when our team was on defense, so though we would miss some of my niece's boyfriend's playing time, I figured we wouldn't miss too much, aka a touchdown.

I hurriedly pushed Julia to the bathroom, and as we both sat down on our thrones, we heard a loud cheery roar from the crowd. At this point, I was frustrated because it sounded as though we had missed something big and I gave Julia a hard time, which I quickly regretted because if she had to go, she had to go. But then it took Julia forever to go because she knew I was disappointed. By this time there was no need to hurry. The crowd's roar had diminished, and I told her to take her time.

When we finally got back to our seats, Nellie excitedly announced, "You missed it! You missed it!"

"What did we miss?" we both asked simultaneously.

"Your cousin's boyfriend ran the ball in for a defensive touchdown!"

It had definitely been the wrong time to go to the bathroom. But at least we were able to see the replay on the news and had a funny story to tell afterward.

Because Julia enjoyed watching sports live so much, I couldn't help but wish she had more time to do it after school and attend more high school games. But the homework load at Helias often made it impossible. Even with my guidance, it took her hours every night to get it all completed. "This is so dumb!" she'd say. We were both exhausted! Eventually, they reduced the amount of homework she had in each class, which did help.

Another one of her least favorite moments was learning to drive. One cool yet sunny fall weekend we were working on the front yard landscaping to beautify our home. My husband drove the Gator around, which hauled the tools, mulch, trim, and some bushes. This gave me a big idea! "We should help Julia try to drive the Gator today."

Initially, we had purchased the little vehicle to not only get around our property but also so that Julia could practice driving with it. The Gator was equipped with hand controls for her, but so far, she had only ever ridden around in the passenger seat. This afternoon, Julia was already in the passenger seat watching us work, so I asked her if she wanted to try to drive.

"No!" Julia cried sternly and with determination.

But I proceeded to urge her on with persuasive comments like: "It can't hurt anything to try, and you never know until you try. Someday driving can be your freedom. Someday you won't want your mom driving you around all the time ..."

My husband chimed in too, so pretty soon, she was talked into it and scooted her way over to the driver's seat. Our dog, Jodee, hopped into the passenger seat with her. She always wanted to be in the middle of the action, especially when we were outside.

My husband explained to Julia how to use the hand controls, turn the steering wheel, start and stop, and the different gears. And then, he helped her start the Gator. I mentioned to him that he should ride with her, but he couldn't hear me. He stood right next to the Gator, though, as Julia nervously pushed the gas hand control to go forward.

The Gator didn't go anywhere.

So, we told her to push a little harder. She did and ... it went forward alright! In fact, the Gator proceeded to move so quickly that it hit the front of the house.

Jodee exited her seat quickly. And Julia started to cry.

We made sure she wasn't hurt; it had just scared her. The spasticity in her muscles actually helped her when she crashed because she was so nervous and stiff holding onto the steering wheel that the impact propelled her butt off the seat but just barely, and her hands still held firmly onto the steering wheel. *Thank God!*

We checked the house too and didn't find any damage. But the real damage had already been done. "I'm NEVER DRIVING, EVER!" Julia said. It reminded me of the time she swore off roller coasters after Splash Mountain at Disney World.

My shoulders dropped. *Oh crap, I ruined this for her.* I had always deeply hoped Julia would drive one day. It was one of those milestones I held quietly in my heart because I knew the kind of freedom and confidence it might bring her. So I couldn't help but mull over the failed situation as we finished our yard work and wished I had made it a more positive experience.

Later, when she was about 18, just to get a base assessment, Julia agreed to go to the Columbia RUSK Rehabilitation Center, which conducted the assessment for disabled people. She had a difficult time during it, so I wasn't surprised when Julia's test came back low on the reflexive portion and her unconverged eyes inhibited her from seeing fully.

Sadly — for me at least — she was deemed unable to drive, for now. This didn't hurt her feelings at all. It scared her to drive. But I told her "maybe someday." There was always the possibility we'd try a new therapy that would help her overcome these physical barriers, and I couldn't give up hoping for that.

"Remember your word to your servant; you have given me hope through it. This is my comfort in my affliction; Your promise has given me life." (Psalms 119:49-50)

CHAPTER 25

On our second trip to Florida for Julia's craniosacral therapy, we met Ann Marie. Her cousin Cecile was receiving treatment after she survived a plane crash. The moment we connected, something just clicked. Ann Marie had this calming, open-hearted energy, and she immediately took an interest in Julia. Not out of obligation, but out of genuine care. She became a dear friend.

During this visit in 2007, we were also told about a certain type of craniosacral therapy in the Bahamas. This treatment is done by massage therapists trained in CST and includes wild dolphins. Apparently the dolphins swim right next to the client and therapist while in the water, and this can release blocked energy.

We decided to go and make it a vacation for the whole family, especially since we were celebrating Emily graduating high school. Her cousin, Chelsey, came along with us, which added to the fun.

We had a terrible flight there as we had to pass through a storm to get to the islands. The plane circled for a little while and then dropped quickly. It had all of us squealing and grabbing hold of one another, while the plane cracked and squeaked. Thank goodness the seatbelt held us down. Julia said her stomach was in her throat, but when I looked at Chelsey and Emily, they were giggling like it was a roller coaster ride. I was grateful I only had one child in panic mode!

When we finally landed, we had to stay on the plane until the storm passed. Then there was 18 inches of water on the tarmac, so we had to wait a little longer than other passengers until the attendants could bring the handicapped chair to deboard Julia. I was glad for the wait because it gave the water a chance to recede, but we still walked through 12 inches of standing water to the airport.

The Bahamas were beautiful even after the storm. We saw a rainbow hanging over the palm trees, which were blowing in the tropical, humid island breeze. We were all hoping for a relaxing week, and that's definitely what we got, but it was also more eventful than any of us thought it would be! On one of our first days there, we noticed a bus pull up outside of our hotel. The people who deboarded were all dressed in historic pirate gear with hats and even eye patches.

When we asked the hotel staff about it, they said another *Pirates of the Caribbean* film was being shot in the area! Unfortunately, we didn't see any of the main cast, but we did sit on some benches outside the hotel another evening, hoping to catch a glimpse of some of them as they got off the bus again.

The CST dolphin therapy was even more memorable. Julia was provided a tight scuba wetsuit that she squirmed into before getting into the water. Even with the wetsuit on, it was cold, which made her body stiffer than normal, but the therapy allowed her to experience some emotional releases. Her head and facial features became relaxed again as they always did with CST too. But nothing could beat having dolphins join in on the therapy. Julia couldn't believe it when a dolphin almost dunked her underwater! She didn't like it.

While Julia was in therapy one afternoon, Emily, Chelsey and I also spent time with the dolphins and booked a Swim with the Dolphin excursion. We took a boat ride to the same alcove where Julia received treatment and where wild dolphins would frequently swim. We watched as the guides gave the dolphins basic commands. Then, not only were the girls able to touch their slick, wet and rubbery skin, but they were also directed by our guides to hold onto the fins. When they did, the dolphins would take them for a swim. If they went too far away, they would then let go of the fin and swim back to the guides, the dolphins swimming back with them so that they could play again. We swam with the dolphins for an hour, and the girls couldn't stop smiling. It was a once-in-a-lifetime experience!

During our stay in the Bahamas, one of the therapists told us about Myofascial Release Therapy (MFR) too. Like many of the therapies I heard about, I read through the brochure's information and then filed it away until a couple years had passed by and I pulled it out again.

MFR is a technique that applies gentle and sustained pressure to the myofascial connective tissues. This gentle pressure along with the slow application of it allows fascia, a viscoelastic medium, to elongate, which helps eliminate pain in and restore motion to patients.

Even though MFR is similar to CST, it added a layer of treatment that CST did not utilize. Sometimes unwinding takes place during which the body remembers (tissue memory) the exact position it was in when the trauma happened and freezes in that position until a release occurs. MFR is able to help the body let go of the fascia restriction that binds the body in pain.

When I talked to a physical therapist at Therapy on the Rocks, he explained that this therapy can release more trauma with every layer it reaches, similar to an onion. Through it, therapists can keep going deeper for greater changes. This meant we had to try it. As always with Julia's therapy, I couldn't stay in the shallows.

Fifth Alternative Treatment: Myofascial Release Therapy (MFR)

In 2008, Julia attended a 2-week intensive treatment of MFR in Sedona, Arizona. We flew into Phoenix first before hopping on a tiny plane that would take us to Flagstaff, where we would have to rent a car. The flight took place right before sunset, and the pilot was kind enough to wave the wings so that we could see the beautiful red rocks below. They were spectacular!

However, Julia became anxious, whether from the tipping plane or the feeling of claustrophobia on the small plane, and started to cry a very unusual high-pitched cry. In any flight, it is frustrating when a child cries, but this? It was disturbing because she was older, and I felt so bad for her and the other passengers. Also, I didn't know how to help her. So, I simply held her whole body as tightly as I could. I talked with her and tried to enjoy the view, but I don't think she ever looked out the window. Needless to say, we were both happy when the plane landed.

Even though Julia's anxious episodes continued to pop their ugly heads out at times, she still had a special charisma about her that intrigued people, and our first visit to the Myofascial Release clinic in Sedona was no different. The top-notch therapists there, who were from all different parts of the country, only wanted what was best for the clients and gave them the utmost care. They made the facility feel like home, and it was comfortable and quiet, so Julia was able to let go of many emotionally charged releases during the sessions. One of the therapists, Judy Bradbury Raugawitz, coincidentally was from Missouri, so Julia bonded with her the most and we became friends.

Julia never met a stranger outside of the clinic as well, and these instances always reminded me of my dad who also had an outgoing personality. We were at a Hampton Inn and had gone to the main lobby for breakfast. Usually we'd be eating and, sure enough, Julia would say hello to a vacationer on another patron at a table nearby. Well, on one particular morning, she rolled over to the table occupied by a husband and wife.

The woman saw the worry on my face as I hoped Julia wasn't disturbing their morning, but she returned a kind, reassuring look to say it was okay. I finished eating and joined them. We visited for a while and, the next thing you know, traded phone numbers and planned to meet them for dinner later in the week.

It was a very nice evening, and we stayed in contact with them for a while after that trip. They both said that if we were ever in their area in Florida, they would be upset if we didn't call and stay with them. What a great – and sweet — meet! We had found some lifelong friends, all because Julia had rolled over to say, "Good morning!"

"The steadfast love of the Lord never ceases, his mercies never come to an end; they are new every morning; great is your faithfulness."

(Lamentations 3:22-23)

CHAPTER 26

WE MADE THE TRIP to the MFR therapy clinic a few times after our first visit, but since the flight to Sedona was dreadful for Julia, I decided to drive there and back for the other treatment sessions. Usually, we left around noon the first day and stayed in Oklahoma. The next day was a long, boring, and straight drive to Albuquerque, New Mexico, and the last day was a short 5-hour jaunt to Sedona.

During one trip, Julia and I were heading to Albuquerque and singing along to a Shania Twain CD. Julia always teased me because I "know the words to none of the songs," but I sang anyway, and every incorrect phrase brought on lots of giggles. While belting out one of Shania's famous hits, though, there was also a little voice inside my head that told me I should turn on the radio instead.

"I want to listen to the radio for a little bit," I told Julia.

"Nooooo," she whined but then gave in because I explained I wanted to listen to the weather forecast.

When the weatherman came on, he announced that there could be 13 inches of snow falling in Flagstaff and Sedona starting at 2 a.m. And that I-17 would likely be closed.

Oh my gosh, I thought, *we need to get there before the storm hits!*

I estimated our total day's drive time to be about 15 hours if I drove straight through. I hadn't gone that long before with no break, but I did not want to get stuck in New Mexico and Julia to miss her treatment. While I put the pedal to the metal, Julia dialed our hotel to see if they would take us early. They found a room, though it wasn't accessible, so we would have to move to the accessible room when it was available the next day, but that was good enough for me. So, with a heaviness on my shoulders upon realizing the long day I had ahead of me, I canceled our hotel reservation in New Mexico and kept driving.

We made it to Flagstaff around 11 p.m. (no snow yet!), but we were both already exhausted. Julia was complaining about her tail bone hurting and that her butt was numb. I told her to wiggle around and kick her legs. My eyes were burning at this point and getting quite drowsy, so I rolled down the window, allowing the crisp air to blow on me.

From Flagstaff, I chose I-17S, a longer route, rather than 89A South because though in the daytime 89A is very beautiful, at night the curvy road would be very taxing on a tired me. But wouldn't you know, they were doing construction on that route. The speed limit was lower than usual, and this extended our time an extra half hour.

We were never happier to see a hotel (except maybe after the trip from hell to Futures Unlimited years before). When we arrived, they had a welcoming basket for Julia and me, which was so sweet! We had gotten to know the hotel staff from a prior stay, so I called the front desk to thank them because it sure warmed my heart and lightened my spirit before we both collapsed onto our beds.

The next morning, we woke to ... 13 inches of snow. It was just as it had been forecasted, and I-17 was closed. I was relieved we had made the right decision and endured the long trip; this also allowed us to take our time the next morning.

Later that day the sun shone bright and melted the snow quicker than it melts in the Midwest, allowing us to get out and buy some groceries for our stay. I was glad to have the full day to relax and prepare for the week and was sure happy I had listened to my little voice!

This was just one of our priceless memories from driving to and from Sedona. Another time when we were there I had recently become curious about vegan food. There was a quaint restaurant I had noticed that was all vegan dishes, so I talked Julia into trying it.

We walked inside with apprehension and stared up at the menu, which had been written on a large blackboard. Having been raised on a farm and a meat lover, I discovered that none of it looked very appetizing. Julia was also skeptical knowing her mom was stepping out of the box (again!), but we both decided on a black bean burger and took our seats.

We were hungry, and it took a little longer to be served than we hoped, but once we were, Julia took one look at the "burger" and didn't want to eat it. I understood because the burger sitting in front of me definitely didn't look like a burger, but I said, "You have to at least try it. Otherwise, you won't know if you really like it or not." Leading by example, I lifted the burger and took a bite.

After chewing for a bit, I sputtered out, "It is ... interesting!" But I think my facial expression said it all. No, it was not the best, but I'm sure it was good in terms of vegan quality. I encouraged Julia to take a bite, but she was adamant about not trying it. As usual, though, I spent time talking her into it and finally watched her put part of the burger into her mouth and then... spit it out.

I started giggling. It was too funny not to, though I glanced around and hoped nobody behind the counter saw her do it.

"It tastes like mulch!!" Julia cried with disgust.

We both started laughing out loud then while still trying to not make a scene. Julia refused to take another bite, and I didn't want to finish mine either, which was unusual for me because I *love* most foods.

The price of vegan food was outrageous at the time, so I wasn't especially happy about that money going down the drain. However, there was nothing left to do but pay and slip out as nonchalantly as possible, which was futile because we were both still laughing, tears rolling down our cheeks, about the burgers tasting like mulch, and they would see that our plates had barely been touched when they cleaned up the table.

Well, we got back in the van, talked about where we wanted to go because we were so hungry by this time we could eat our foot, and sure enough, we landed at McDonalds! Yes, the exact opposite in cuisine. We were still laughing as we dug into our greasy beef patties and french fries. A fond and fun memory of trying something new and experiencing life and every penny was worth it.

With Julia in therapy every day, this meant I had some time to myself, and I made the most of it. I went to some conferences for the continuing education portion of my massage therapy license, took hikes to see if I could feel the vortexes, and went on a Pink Jeep Tour. I even made an appointment with a gentleman who said he could hear from Jesus and Mary during his sessions.

How interesting! I've never heard of someone hearing from Jesus and Mary in this way. Because I was of the Catholic faith, I wondered if I would be doing something wrong, but my curiosity won out. *Surely it can't be a bad thing.*

The man's office was very inviting with jute hangings, linen cloth on the windows, and plants everywhere. The man himself had long sandy blond hair. He was thin but healthy looking, gentle in nature but quite engaging.

After I had made myself comfortable, he asked if there was anything in my life that I wanted to know more about or areas in which I would like some spiritual direction. I didn't share much. Not only was I a shy and private person at times, but I wanted to let this time be as natural as possible.

During the hour-long session, the man told me some general information about my marriage; it didn't surprise me but confirmed my own thoughts and feelings. Toward the end, he said that Mary told him I needed to sing. This resonated with me the most. I loved to sing, but somehow that activity rarely happened, except when I was at Mass. Years ago, I had sung with the special voice class in high school and then to the girls before bedtime. I was also a bass with the Sweet Adelines, a singing group, for about nine months before I had to quit because I didn't have time for it and everything else. I wondered if singing would be a part of my future and when it would happen.

This wasn't the only unique experience I planned during our Arizona trips. In fact, if you want to try other "spiritual practices" or want to know about anything outside of religion, like healing modalities, you will find it in Sedona. There was a palm reader on every strip mall and brochures galore at the hotels. One brochure stood out to me. It had a Native American man on the front. Inside it discussed a type of shamanic healing that could bring balance back to the mind and body through astrological consultation and breathing exercises.

As always, I was searching for what the world had to offer outside of the healing modalities I already understood, and I was intrigued. *What else can I find out about myself through this unique practice?* So, I called for an appointment and explained that I had never done anything like this type of healing before but wanted to find out more. This man also had a gentle voice and took time to discuss it all with me. By the end of the conversation, I felt I could trust him and booked a session.

He had availability that week while Julia was in treatment and said we needed about two hours total for travel and the healing practice. He also said he would pick me up at the hotel where I was staying and drive us out to a "power spot" to have the session. For some reason, I was not the least bit alarmed for my safety. However, even as a grown adult, I would have never told my mother I was doing this.

We hung up, and I thought, *What am I doing?* But then I told myself I was merely stepping out of the box I was in to experience something that I normally would not. *It's good for me to do things like this*, I reassured myself.

The shaman pulled into the hotel the next morning in an old Suburban-type truck, and when I shook hands with him and looked into his eyes (which was unusual for me to do) while introductions were exchanged, I was suddenly calm. My nervousness almost disappeared. About 10 minutes into the drive, though, I would be lying if I said I didn't have some apprehension or question if this was a good idea or not. I did. But, the man didn't give me any reason to mistrust him, and I felt drawn to him spiritually in some odd way. *Surely, a brochure would not be marketed if this was not a trustworthy and professional man.*

When we arrived at the "power spot," he got out of the truck and pulled out a Native American-style blanket. He said we would sit on it under a Juniper tree nearby. We walked for about five minutes through the rugged rocks and cacti, small plants, and medium-sized Juniper trees. If at any point I needed to direct myself back to the vehicle, I could not.

We made it to the place, he set out the blanket and asked me to sit down. I did. It was hot, and the tree didn't provide a lot of shade, but I wasn't going to complain. Instead, I wanted to ask questions, but as I began my inquiry, he gently said, "This is our meditation time." So, I quit talking.

Awkward silence. We, or really just *he* meditated for maybe 5-10 minutes. I had never, except while at the Motherhouse, experienced so much silence in my life! Finally, he requested that I take some deep breaths and began teaching me some breathing exercises. After this, he talked about the heavens, astrology signs, houses, gatekeepers, and the planets. All this was foreign to me and didn't make much sense. I didn't understand how this would help me.At the end of the session, he picked up the blanket and walked back to the truck. It was fairly quiet. I didn't have many questions because when I did, I didn't understand his answers. But two things he shared that I would never forget was that I wouldn't be married much longer and that I'd be rich. Rich in what? I didn't know. Was it love, money, or spiritual richness? Perhaps the next few years would answer this question.

When he dropped me off at the hotel, I took out my wallet to pay him and thanked him. I felt in some way a wall had been broken down, but I couldn't explain what wall or how it had come down. The shaman sent me his reading later, but I didn't keep it.

However, this wasn't the end of my spiritual curiosity. A sweet gal who Julia befriended at a Sedona hotel mentioned an astrologer in the state of Washington. She said that many elite people see her, which told me I wouldn't be able to afford a session with her. When I returned home, though, I called the astrologer anyway, and the cost wasn't as bad as I thought it would be. I booked an appointment, which would be held over the phone. By now I was working full time.

The session lasted an hour and consisted of more astrology language I didn't understand. The woman also told me things about my life. Some of the information was general that could apply to anyone; other parts of it were not. For instance, she said I would meet someone after my divorce (which was interesting because the Shaman also told me I would get divorced), and though it would not last long, I would marry him. I asked, "Do you have a name?" She gave it to me. I was perplexed because I didn't know anyone by that name and afterward even forgot the name she said.

But as with all the spiritual informants I had met with in Sedona, I did wonder if any of what they said would come to pass. Or if these foretellings were simply for curious people like me looking for answers.

I never frequented any other types of healing sessions in this realm again, and I didn't pull Julia into any of it either. Eventually, even Julia's MFR sessions in Sedona weren't beneficial enough to make the long drives we took worth it. They were beneficial in that she experienced an emotional release while there, though I wasn't sure if crying releases were good for her, but her physical movements weren't any better. Many people attended Therapy on the Rocks and received great healing from different traumas, but this wasn't the case for Julia.

Both CST and MFR were beneficial, but the effects did not last as cerebral palsy is its own animal. I had so hoped MFR would be the treatment that helped her rise up to her feet at least temporarily. I had prayed, *God, will you do it?* I wanted for Julia what her sister had: something ordinary. A normal teenage life with late nights, friend drama, and independence. But Julia's story was different from other people's, and although it would continue to be, the most important thing was that it was just as sweet because every moment of grace felt like a quiet triumph.

"Certainly, there is a future, and your hope will not be cut off."

(Proverbs 23:18)

Chapter 27

Before I knew it, it was Julia's senior year of high school. We were sitting on the court sidelines at one of the basketball games as we always did. At halftime, the coach stood up and the team gathered around him. He announced that they wanted to recognize their most valued fan ... Julia!

Julia looked at me in shock and I looked at her with a big smile across my face. "Go up there!" I urged her. I wasn't going with her to accept it. "It's for you." Julia was overwhelmed, her heart feeling like it could pound out of her chest. She rolled out onto the court, and they presented her with the "Fan of the Year" award and a basketball signed by the whole team. A few years before, the volleyball team had given her a signed ball too. These kind gestures were not small to Julia. They were huge! They were reminders that she was seen, appreciated, and celebrated — *not* because of what she couldn't do but because of exactly who she was.

When the senior prom arrived that spring, sweet Emily came back from college and took her to the dance. Julia was surprised, and it was a huge surprise to me too because they typically didn't talk much when they were both at home. But Emily helped Julia with her hair and dress, and they had a wonderful night. For me, as a mom, this was a highlight. I had always had a close relationship with my sister and wanted my daughters' relationship with each other to blossom into that same sisterly love.

Graduation came quickly after that. It was held at the packed St. Joseph Cathedral, the same spot as Emily's graduation two years before. For Julia, it was a "finally" feeling. She didn't want to see inside another school ever again! After the ceremony, Mrs. Noonan, Julia's favorite teacher, came up to her and handed her a binder. It was titled "Wise Words" and dedicated to "her dear friend Julia who is a fountain of wisdom herself and inspires the lives of many." Julia opened the binder and found that it was filled with all of the quotes she had picked out over the years for Mrs. Noonan's blackboard. Quotes like:

- *"Be a fountain not a drain." (Anonymous)*

- *"One filled with joy preaches without preaching." (Mother Teresa)*

- *"Life isn't about waiting for the storm to pass. It's about learning to dance in the rain." (Vivian Greene)*

- *"Everyone has handicaps except some people's handicaps you can't see. (Marilyn Kay, aka Mom)*

- *"Laughter has no foreign accent." (Paul Lowney)*

- *"The years in your life are less important than the life in your years." (a version of Abraham Lincoln's famous quote)*

It was the sweetest gesture to create a great memory!

The next month would be a big one for Emily too because she turned 21! I knew I wouldn't have much one-on-one time with her because she and her boyfriend seemed to be getting close to an engagement, so I thought it would be best to celebrate her birthday in May. I asked her what she thought about going to New York for a long weekend. "We could get some Broadway musical tickets and see some sights!"

Emily was hesitant at first about the trip, and I wondered if she was deciding how much time she was okay spending with me and how long she was fine being away from her boyfriend. Emily and I had become more and more distant over the past few years, even though I had tried to build more of a relationship with her the summer before she went to college.

She had entered and won 1st Runner-Up in the Cole County Fair Queen contest, receiving $300 for her college tuition. And, together, we had shopped for the perfect dress for the talent portion, gone over her speech several times, and also found a beautiful evening gown for the question-and-answer time. I was so happy to watch her succeed.

There had also been an audition for a play, *The Family Nobody Wanted*, at the Stained Glass Theater, and because I was in a couple of high school musicals like her years ago, I mentioned that we should do it together. She read through the summarized storyline and decided to join me, and I was elated!

But little did I know God was planning something much different. Emily met her future boyfriend, who was also a part of our cast. So I was quickly moved "backstage" in her mind, while she and her boyfriend took the "mainstage" in her world *and* on the actual stage as the lead actors. However, it was an overall great experience, and I was still able to cheer her on as she nailed every performance. I could also watch the relationship between her and her boyfriend bloom from behind the scenes.

Then suddenly it was August, and we were moving her into a college freshman dorm at Stephens College where she would study to become an actress. After a semester there, however, she decided she didn't want to be an actress. The program felt too competitive, not fun, plus the high tuition costs. She transferred to Missouri State University to study Early Childhood Education, but once she got into the classroom, she realized that having summers off wasn't worth the toll of being in a classroom all day and working on lesson plans in the evenings. So she changed her major to Child and Family Development with an emphasis in Family Studies.

Unfortunately, moving her belongings to Missouri State — something that should have been easy and exciting — was tainted by a stressful situation. As I was driving to the campus, with Emily following behind me, I briefly looked for my next turn. When I looked back at the road, I realized the car in front of me had stopped. I slammed on the brakes so hard I think my foot touched the floorboard. Then CLUNK! CLUNK! My heart sank as I felt the three-car collision.

Thankfully, I had stopped in the "nick of time" because nobody was hurt. I only gave the vehicle in front of me a fiberglass tear in the bumper from my license plate that was slightly damaged. But Emily's car would need a few small repairs. We called the police and waited as they took our information. A lot of deep sighs later, we were able to move Emily into the dorm.

As I drove home afterward, I was a little sad realizing Emily would be a couple hours away. My little girl was all grown up! What I didn't realize was how much more emotionally distant she and I would become.

Sadly, she doesn't remember me calling her much while she was in school; I was just so preoccupied with Julia and work. She didn't call either, unless she needed something, and I was always glad to help when I could. We did go shopping together one weekend, and another time she invited Julia and me to a Fresh Grounded Faith Christian conference. The praise and worship was outstanding, and the speakers were very inspirational. Plus all three of us love stand-up comedy. Tim Hawkins was one the highlights of the event, and he didn't disappoint us! Julia had to purchase all his CDs afterward.

We enjoyed seeing Emily, but I didn't know what to talk to her about, even when she came home for the holidays. She would spend most of her time hanging out with friends, which I thought was normal for her age, but I knew there was more to it than that. We were distanced, kept unintentionally distracted; not only by miles but heart as well. I hated it.

So when it came time to celebrate her 21st birthday, I really wanted to experience a special trip with her to help our relationship. To ensure there were no snags in the travel plans, I called our favorite travel agency, and they set us up in a hotel near Times Square.

We arrived in New York City later than expected, and the ride into Manhattan felt like we were moving in slow motion. *We're not going fast enough to make our hotel check-in,* I worried. Every light began to make me anxious because everything hinged on the city traffic and our hopefully competent taxi driver. And it was rush hour.

We did make it to our hotel within an okay window of time, but then when we talked to the staff at the hotel's front desk, they couldn't find our reservation. *We don't have a room in New York!? But where will we go?* I began to panic internally. *We CAN'T miss the show tonight, and this trip CAN'T have any problems. It just can't.*

With tears in my eyes, I pleaded with the reception staff. "Our reservation has to be here. It was made through my travel agent! We're celebrating my daughter's 21st birthday, and we're supposed to be at our first musical tonight by 7:30 for the 8 p.m. show. Please, there has to be something you can do."

The initial representative hesitated with me at least twice by saying, "I'm sorry, ma'am, we don't have a room left!" and I watched the clock strike 6:30 p.m. *We'll never make it!* I pleaded with them again. She finally spoke with a manager on duty and then informed us they found a corner room. I was relieved and thanked them over and over. As an apology, they did send up a bottle of champagne for

Emily's birthday. It was nice, but she didn't drink alcohol much at this point and I didn't like champagne. However, the room had to have been nicer than the one that the travel agency had booked because there was a 90-degree corner window overlooking Times Square.

We took in the view quickly, then dressed for the first musical, *Mamma Mia!*, and arrived just minutes before the doors closed. *Whew!* I looked at Emily, and we both started giggling with relief. This was the one Broadway musical that we both really wanted to see, so I had splurged and grabbed up floor seating about 10 rows from the stage. And, we loved it! It was the perfect show for a mom and daughter. The talent was exceptional, and the music was amazing (as always). *There's no way another show could outdo this one*, I thought. But there were still more to come.

We saw three more shows while we were in New York: *Wicked*, *Jersey Boys*, and *Rock of Ages*. In between these performances, we took the double-decker hop-on-hop-off bus to the Statue of Liberty, the Empire State Building (we didn't care to go all the way up though), St. Patrick's Cathedral, and the Diamond district.

We walked to Central Park and decided to try a pedicab. The man promised he would have us back on time for our evening show, so Emily and I loaded into the back seat. He was a fantastic tour guide! I especially enjoyed hearing about the areas in the park where specific movies were filmed, including the *Friends* fountain, buildings in *GhostBusters,* and the bridge from *Home Alone 2.*

I'll admit, New York City seemed smaller than we imagined. Even the building for *The Tonight Show* starring David Letterman seemed underwhelming. The street food didn't appeal to us, but we did enjoy the pizza at John's Pizzeria of Times Square. It was the best pizza we'd ever had!

Although neither of us cared for the busyness, crowds and the dirty city, it was exciting to be first-time visitors experiencing the lights on Broadway. (*Mamma*

Mia! was the best musical, by the way!) I treasured this time and especially hoped Emily had fun, but I did worry that when we made it back home, our relationship would be the same as it had always been. She had to give her attention to school and her soon-to-be fiance, and my focus would be on my job and a newly graduated Julia.

"There is nothing better for a man than that he should eat and drink and find enjoyment in his toil. This also, I saw, is from the hand of God." (Ecclesiastes 2:24)

PART 4

CHAPTER 28

WHEN JULIA FINISHED HIGH school, I told her she wasn't going to sit around and do nothing all day. I had been raised on our family farm where there was always something to get done, and if we weren't busy, we were given something to do. Mom would say, "Hey, while you're sitting there, pod these peas, or snip these beans, or fold these clothes, or take this slop (the kitchen scraps) to the hogs."

We were always busy, and I wanted to raise my girls with a similar mentality. Number one, that they could do whatever they set their minds to; number two, that they had a purpose; and number three, that they should work hard and always do their best. And hopefully it would be at a job they loved.

After Julia graduated, I encouraged her to keep volunteering at the Special Learning Center, where she had attended preschool. During her senior year at Helias, she had started helping there as part of her required Christian service hours. Now, with school behind her, she could help more often, three days a week. She enjoyed being there. She liked helping the teachers, playing with the kids, especially because, deep down, part of her still wanted to be a kid.

Debbie was still the director and was in charge of organizing the center's biggest fundraiser. Earlier, it started with the Jefferson City Cosmopolitan Club who held the Tom Henke Classic then they added the Banquet to raise money for the club and the Special Learning Center later. That year, she started inviting former students to share music or give speeches about what the Special Learning Center meant to them. Since Julia was already volunteering and had such a strong connection with the center, Debbie thought she'd be a perfect speaker.

The banquet was held at the Capitol Plaza Hotel, the nicest venue in Jefferson City. Tom Henke had invited several Cardinal baseball players to attend such as: Ozzie Smith, Joe Buck, Scott Bailes, Danny Cox, Ken Dayley, Charlie James, and others. During the event, a previous student played music, and there was a celebrity impersonator, and our famous Rod Smith, our local Rod's Big Ol Fish sportscaster.

After these people it was Julia's turn. She received the cue to move toward the stage's ramp, and I heard her sigh. I gave her a pat on her leg and a little push and told her, "You can do this." She made her way to Debbie and faced the crowd of about 350. Then she froze.

The silence stretched on. It felt like forever because Julia is usually never at a loss for words. As I sat there watching and anticipating her to start, I was taking deep breaths for her, silently praying, asking God to help her take a deep breath and center herself.

Debbie gave Julia a couple of gentle prompts of encouragement. Then finally, Julia began to read with the microphone in one hand and her speech in the other. But after just a sentence or two, the paper in her hand was shaking so badly her eyes couldn't keep their place. Debbie quietly asked if she wanted help holding the microphone, and once Debbie took it, Julia could read easier, steadying the paper with both hands.

Her courage was unmistakable. And when she finished, the heartfelt crowd gave her a standing ovation, not just for the speech, but also for her bravery in pushing through the fear and finishing what she came to do.

Afterward, she came up to me, and I said, "You did so well!" I gave her a congratulatory hug and could feel her heart still beating so hard that her whole body was moving. I squeezed her tighter to help calm her and told her I was so proud of her for getting up there and telling her important story.

Later, Debbie told me that Julia's moment on stage made her feel *real* to the attendees. And because of Julia's speech, Debbie and her team from the JC Cosmopolitan Club and the Special Learning Center's board members' hard work, and many attendees' generosity, the banquet raised one of the largest donations ever, about $55,000. Needless to say, the night was a success in many ways!

After about a year volunteering at the Special Learning Center, Julia then took on a job through Capitol Projects Inc.

Capitol Projects provided work opportunities for the physically, mentally, and behaviorally disabled. I was proud of her for saying yes to the position, but honestly, I also didn't want to believe my daughter needed to work there. To me, Julia's abilities didn't match the jobs she did at a sheltered workshop-type workplace since her disability was mostly physical. I believed her to be not only more capable but also worth more than the $2.30 she made an hour. Plus, the mental and behavioral challenges of the other employees increased her anxiety, and my heart quickly broke for her. Yet she took the Handi-Wheels bus each day and pressed onward.

By the next May in 2011, Julia needed a break. And I did too. So we used my vacation time I had accrued and planned a trip together to Florida to visit some friends we had met on our previous travels.

Our first stop was St. Louis. We like baseball and had bought two tickets to see the St. Louis Cardinals play. The Cardinals won, and Julia said we were their good luck charms! The next day we saw Ralphie May's stand-up comedy show in Paducah, Kentucky.

Then came the long day of travel to St. Augustine, Florida, to see the friends we had met in Sedona that one morning when Julia had rolled over to say "good morning." Some years ago, the husband and wife had lost their 11-year-old son, who had also been diagnosed with cerebral palsy, and said he had a similar personality as Julia. So they were completely charmed by her. We spent the day relaxing at their amazingly beautiful home and then had a little lunch before going shopping in a nice shopping district.

The next morning, after a hearty southern breakfast, we headed further south to visit Ann Marie and her husband, Ty. On the way to their home near West Palm Beach, these black bugs I had never seen before continuously pelted the windshield. After a while, it seemed like they were raining from the sky, and I couldn't see the road very well. Like many other drivers, we stopped at a gas station, and I tried to clean it off the best I could with a squeegee despite the water container being empty. Then we set out again, but the bugs were relentless, and our windshield was soon covered once more.

We arrived at Ann Marie and Ty's house and shared a round of hugs, and then Ann Marie quickly noticed our vehicle. They told us they were called "love bugs."

"Well, I definitely wasn't feeling the 'love,'" I replied with a chuckle. Ty immediately showed his southern hospitality and pulled out his garden hose to spray off the car and then took it to the car wash for a second cleaning.

We stayed the weekend with them and had such a fun visit. Like our friends in St. Augustine, Ann Marie's hospitality was over the top, and Ty made some salmon and king crab legs one evening (our favorite). Ann Marie also made us lemon drop martinis, but they were too strong for both Julia and me, so we told her to enjoy hers. And she did!

The next day, we went to the beach together. It was difficult to get Julia out of the sand and into her chair, but a couple of young, good-looking men came to the rescue. Like angels, they picked her up and carried her to her wheelchair, and I made a comment to Julia that "God always seems to have your back, doesn't He?!" She just giggled, and then we let the guys know how grateful we were for their help.

It came time for us to leave Ann Marie and Ty, which was bittersweet, but we had to return home so I could get back to work. On our way back from Florida, we stayed in a town in Alabama before making our way to Lexington, Kentucky. There, we visited the Louisville Slugger baseball bat factory. Julia loved it. She was fascinated by the whole process of the bats being carved and finished. After that, we drove home.

The trip had been full of unexpected memories — the beach, bugs, baseball, and blessings — and it left our hearts full.

Later that fall, Ann Marie flew into Missouri to celebrate Julia's 21st birthday. We made the trek to Hermann, a German town, where we spread out a blanket on the grass in the sunshine and enjoyed cheese, crackers, and wine while listening to the cheerful German music. Then we celebrated with family and friends and ate BBQ. Julia drank a little beer and enjoyed her ice cream cake. We loved the precious time we shared with our dear friend and looked forward to seeing her again. Also, I hoped the trip to Florida and spending time with good people like Ann Marie would be beneficial for Julia. They seemed to ease the anxiousness she typically felt from work for a short time.

While Julia was finding her way in the workplace, Emily had taken a big step in her relationship ... She was getting married! Her boyfriend proposed to her during her senior year of college, so it was time to plan the wedding. However, it was difficult for her to do that while being out of town and studying so much, so this was my chance to help her and, ultimately, reconnect with her again.

My sweet sister-in-law, Amy, volunteered to lend a hand, not surprisingly. It was one of our favorite things to do together: design anything from floral arrangements to house plans to home decor. We made Emily's wedding flower bouquets in my basement and all the beautiful table arrangements for the reception. I would send Emily pictures of what we were thinking to get her input. She had some suggestions, but mostly she would say, "Mom, just do it!" And I would. I just wanted her to be happy with her special day!

But the most exciting part for me was going wedding dress shopping. As a young mother, I had dreamed about watching my girls pick out their white gowns. I had gotten a taste of this with Emily when she picked out her senior prom dress. It was the most beautiful prom gown I had ever seen, and Emily LOVED it. Blue with a teal overlay, it was strapless and the bodice was heavily adorned with sequins, which made it sparkle all over. I spent $500 for that dress and had to remind myself that we found her junior prom dress for $15 the year before.

However, the day we bought the dress was also the same day the Knights of Columbus Sweetheart Dinner and Dance was held, which included lotteries that could be won throughout the evening. We ended up winning $500, and it was then I announced to her dad that the amount was the exact amount we had paid for the dress! My poor husband. He grimaced and rolled his eyes, but at least his daughter was happy!

Three years later, I was hoping to see Emily have that same satisfied and overjoyed look on her face that she had when she found her prom dress. But this time it would be because of her perfect wedding dress.

The saleslady brought out three to four dresses for us to see that were in our price range. I was excited for Emily to try them all on, but the thought definitely didn't cross my mind that she would find the perfect dress among the selection. In fact, I anticipated we wouldn't find it even after shopping for a couple of *days*.

The first one Emily tried on was, meh! The second one really appealed to Emily when she saw it on the rack and ... she LOVED it! I watched her face light up once again as she looked at herself in the mirror, and when she found out it had pockets, she started jumping up and down! The elegant dress was made of satin fabric and strapless with a simple A-line skirt. A row of sequins and jewels adorned and shimmered on the top and bottom of the broad pleated tuxedo waistline. The look was complete with a combed netting veil. She tried on more dresses to appease me — she knew I was a bit deflated that more shopping wouldn't be happening — but I could tell she really didn't want to. She had found THE dress, and that made me happy.

The wedding was set for January 7, 2012. I was wary of the timing as Emily was graduating in early December and her fiance still had one more semester to go, but they wanted to be married during the holiday break. So, January 7 it was! God took care of us again. It was an unbelievable, gorgeous 62-degree day! I was so happy for Emily and that she would be starting this new exciting journey of marriage.

Planning for her wedding had been a great distraction from my crumbling marriage, and after 25 years together and seeking counseling (for myself), my ex-husband and I had ended it. Well, it had ended long before emotionally, but the papers were officially signed in September 2011.

It was no surprise to either of my girls, but that didn't make it any easier. I was sad and heartbroken, yet at the same time, there was a sense of freedom and relief. A priest once told me marriage isn't supposed to be a prison.

As a result of the divorce, the house I had designed was now too big for just Julia and me, so we sold it and moved in with a friend for a short time until we moved to our own place. But this is when things really took a turn for the worse.

"Having the eyes of your hearts enlightened, that you may know what is the hope to which he has called you, what are the riches of his glorious inheritance in the saints."

(Ephesians 1:18)

CHAPTER 29

BY HER EARLY 20S, Julia's mood changes were more prevalent and her "episodes," similar to the ones she went through in high school, were gradually increasing. She put on a good front to the outside world, but I'd often wonder what I would come home to: whether it would be the "old" Julia or a sad and somewhat distraught version of her.

She was no longer working at Capitol Projects and had quit because of an unusual traumatic event that occurred in the cafeteria. After it happened, she fled to the bathroom and refused to come out. I couldn't blame her for that. I was called to persuade her to come out, and that was the end of her two years there. After that she worked part time at my office shredding paper for a manager down the hall, which she enjoyed. This work helped her stay busy, and her anxiety was not as prominent there.

Out of love for trying to help us both, some family members thought she was doing it all for attention because many times she was wailing with no tears. Kathy would come over for a while so she wasn't left alone and I could take a walk for some fresh air and a break. When I left the house, Kathy said she would quit crying. When I came back, it would start up again, so I could see their point. But, that didn't stop me from trying to help her in any way that I could.

I remembered all the inspirational quotes Julia had given from Mrs. Noonan in high school, so I wrote positive quotes on paper and placed them on her wall where they would be the first thing she saw when she woke up. But, as you might guess, this seemed to be the last thing she was interested in when she was "deep in it."

I set up home health assistance so someone would be able to stay with her during the day while I worked. But the aide on staff fell asleep on the couch, which caused Julia to miss her psychology appointment. Well, that aide didn't come back, and I was frustrated. It felt like I was searching for a babysitter again.

Thankfully, during this incredibly difficult time, I had a very understanding boss, Chris Buckland. He never made me feel guilty when I needed to leave unexpectedly. He trusted me to make up the hours when I could, and that kind of flexibility was a quiet blessing. It gave me just a little more room to breathe, and I was grateful for that.

By the time she was 23, Julia began to experience more profound episodes, and her "good days" were like her previous "not so great days." She wasn't sleeping well and would cry often; sometimes I even woke up to her sobbing.

I would lie with her some nights to calm her, but the rest of the time, I had to separate myself from it. I'd sleep in my own bed and take showers in the morning, partly so I wouldn't hear her as loudly and partly to prepare myself for another day. Sometimes I would use the noise of the shower to mute my own sobs. It was becoming too much ... for both of us.

Julia and I called Dr. Shipman who said Julia had adrenal exhaustion, and he started to "clear" what was coming up emotionally with her over the phone. Clearing is a prayer said for a client until the muscle testing is "clear" or the symptom is gone. We called Dr. Shipman more and more until we were calling every day and then multiple times per day. The clearings would help briefly, but then the crying would commence again.

One morning I was at my wits' end, and I did something totally out of character. I went into her bedroom and yelled at her to quit crying, hoping this would shock her into stopping. But while I was shouting, something inside me broke and I also shook the bed and then grabbed her by her shoulders and shook her. It wasn't hard enough to hurt her, but it wasn't gentle either. I just wanted her to stop crying. For *all* of it to stop, the helplessness and the heartfelt pain.

Then I saw, *really* saw, her face. My heart shattered and immediately I regretted what I had done and apologized over and over to her. I then held her as tightly as I could, hoping she could feel my love through the mess. "Julia, I don't know how to help you. I just want you to feel better." We both lay there crying.

"Where's Dad?" she asked. "I want Dad." I would do anything for her, so I called him. He came to the apartment and lay down on her bed. He stayed with her for the next few hours patting her back while she rested her head on his chest and listened to his heartbeat, which calmed her down.

As I drove back to work, I mulled over this question in my mind: *How can I expect Julia to know how to handle this when I don't know how to handle it myself?* I was discouraged and depressed by the situation with the weight of it all tears streamed down my face. "God, I need a miracle," I cried out. Please help her, and me!" Internally, I was pleading, *Will you do it?* I was doing my best, but it didn't seem like it was enough this time.

Julia's uncle, aunt, and grandma truly became angels on earth for us. They would invite Julia over to their houses or plan various activities for them to do together. Uncle Wayne, who was a positive male figure in her life, would take her to the YMCA, where she could swim in the mornings. This was a helpful exercise for Julia because it released some of her energy and calmed her.

Sometimes she and Uncle Wayne would also just drive around or stop at Binder Lake, Runge Nature Center, his and Laverne's house, or even McDonald's where they would order fish fries and drinks while reciting funny movie lines when it was appropriate for their day-to-day situations. Usually, they were quotes from *Christmas Vacation*. Like when Cousin Eddie says, "Save the neck for me, Clark," or "Merry Christmas! Shitter was full!" Julia loved it when she got to ride along on the golf cart while Uncle Wayne and Aunt Laverne golfed or watched golf on the TV with them. Aunt Laverne would also take her to her workout classes.

It calmed me knowing Julia was in good hands while I was at work. She was with people she loved and people who loved her. Although it was still a hard time, it was a beautiful one too because so many people were consistently showing up for Julia. It was a good reminder that I should also show up for the other people in my life, not just my daughters, as well.

In the summer of 2013, Robert, a friend from my work, which was now the Department of Mental Health, was going through radiation and chemotherapy due to lung cancer. I would call him before I drove home, and he would ask if I could bring him milkshakes because that is all he'd want to eat.

One night after he had already endured radiation earlier that day, he called and asked if I would take him to the emergency room because he was coughing up blood. I stayed at the hospital until he was released and the doctors gave him some information. He did not share much of the news except that he could choose to go to a university to put a mesh in his lung or go home. Neither option was good.

It was 2 a.m. when I drove him home. The city streets were dark and still, and the air felt heavy. He suddenly broke the silence and said, "I think they are killing me." I did my best to be positive and said, "Oh, Robert, it will be okay!" and told him I would check on him the next morning. It was all I could offer at the moment.

The next day, I called his number. No answer.

I knew that was odd and probably not a good sign. I couldn't ignore the feeling in my chest, so Julia and I went to check on him. I didn't want to leave her home alone.

Robert didn't answer the door. My heart fell and then started to beat louder and louder. If one can feel death around you, I did.

I called the police, and they came shortly after and broke open the door. They returned to our van, where Julia and I were waiting, and informed us that he was found on the floor near the phone and that he had passed. I wished I had fully understood that when he had chosen to go home from the ER, it really meant "go home."

Julia started crying. She said she wanted to go where he went. "WHAT?!" I exclaimed. I moved to the back seat where she was sitting and put my arms around her. "Julia, no you don't!! You belong here, and you are staying here, and it is all going to be ok!"

We drove home. She took a nap. And I desperately yearned for the darkness over us to go away.

"Some sat in darkness, in utter darkness, prisoners suffering in iron chains."

(Psalm 107:10)

CHAPTER 30

IN LIGHT OF ROBERT'S passing, his position in the Department of Mental Health became vacant, and my bosses asked me to fill it. However, I knew nothing about his job and didn't need that stress on top of everything else. My old job became available just at the right time, so I went back to the Department of State Parks, which was an easier transition.

In this role, and the same office I had worked before, I would travel around the state inspecting public parks, counties, cities and the state parks that were considering qualifying for recreational grants. My favorite responsibility was doing a pre-construction site inspection to ensure the plans would follow the grant application and doing the post-site inspection to ensure it was complete before the agency or nonprofit received reimbursement for the expenses incurred. I also met someone during one of my trips. We began to talk and then started long distance dating. Soon he was showing up at my door more and more. We got to know each other, which meant he also got to know Julia.

Eventually, he told me he believed Julia was much brighter than she was letting on, that she was being manipulative because she didn't want us dating, and that she just needed to get over it all. Some of this may have been true, but I knew he didn't understand mental health and I had heard the same concern from some relatives before, so it wasn't anything new. But it was still hard to hear. Meanwhile, Julia's lack of sleep had begun to cause her to have delusional episodes, and I had to ask myself, *Am I going crazy, or is she?*

It all felt like a bad dream!

So, again, during one of Julia's profound events, I called Dr. Shipman and was honest with him. "I don't know what to do anymore. What we are doing isn't helping." True to his nature, gentle but wise, he listened and recommended I take Julia to the emergency room. I agreed. No hesitation.

I wanted Julia to agree to go to the hospital too, but she didn't want to because she "didn't think she would ever get out," she told me later. I explained to her that many people have trouble sleeping and get help for it, and she gave in with the hope that they would prescribe her something to fix the issue. As someone who is against pharma, I wasn't necessarily comfortable with this strategy, but Julia was spiraling into a deep hole, and I didn't know how to get her out of it. So, my soul relented. It seemed like it was the only option we had left.

We drove to the hospital in silence. I tried to be strong for Julia, but there were tears in my eyes and hers. I couldn't believe this was our reality. *What has become of my beautifully spirited daughter, and what will become of her future? I have always done my best for her, but why do I feel like a failure?* As we parked at the emergency room, I prepared to walk us both into the unknown.

There was a *long* wait. And when we finally saw a physician and counselor, of course ... *Here we go again.* I had to leave the room so they could ensure she wasn't being abused. *Deep sigh.* If they only knew how much I loved her! But I understood they had to go through their process to protect her.

When we were reunited, the doctors told us that she could be admitted to find out more about what was going on but that they didn't have a bed on the psychiatric floor. "This means we will need to transfer you to Springfield."

Her whole body was drained, but when Julia heard this, I saw a terror energy show up in her eyes, which were looking directly at me! I knew what she was thinking. She didn't want to go to Springfield. It probably sounded like they were "putting her away." Plus, she would be with people she did not know, and I wouldn't be around if she needed something.

Immediately, my spirit told me that this was not going to happen, and I didn't even have to say a word. The physicians saw her face and mine then pivoted and decided to put her on another floor because she wasn't showing any signs of self-harm. Relieved, she stayed there that night. I hoped they would find out what the issue was and help her.

The night turned into a week. The doctors wanted to do more testing, so a bed was found for her on the psychiatric floor. Although a lot of that time became a blur in my memory, I do remember feeling, honestly, a slight sense of relief because I was able to get more rest. I knew Julia was being taken care of, so it was an emotional break of sorts. I prepared for work that week in silence, something I was grateful to hear, though I was still worried sick about her.

She called me with the hospital phone because she wasn't allowed to have her cell phone and asked me to come to get her. "No, you have to stay for now to go to groups and counseling," I said, trying to stuff down my emotions,

They wouldn't let me visit her until mid-week. When I arrived, Julia was sitting in her wheelchair leaning her arms on the table in front of her. She was very quiet but happy to see me. We hugged, but when she looked at me, I noticed her eyes were dilated and she seemed a little numbed out. She wasn't her old sweet self. Julia would look around her very stealthily and out of the corner of her eye at the other patients who were sitting at other tables or walking around. This look was out of character, and so was her just staring out. She was receiving drugs that would help her anxiety and allow her to fall asleep more easily, so I thought these actions were likely side effects.

"How did I get in here?" she asked me while glancing around at everyone else nearby.

I just said, "Why do *you* think so?"

She answered, "I don't know." Then added, "I don't belong here."

"I don't think you do either," I responded gently, "but for now, you need to be here for a little bit. I do look forward to having you back home, though, and that is our goal, remember?"

I said it all kindly but matter of factly. I believed it would be a wake-up call to how serious her mental health had become mostly from no sleep, which stemmed from anxiety. At the same time, I had to ensure she knew she wasn't being abandoned. I sensed she may be thinking that, and I needed her to know she could trust me, no matter what, throughout the situation.

The next day, Kathy also visited Julia, and they also talked about why she was there. Kathy told me that Julia knew it was her thoughts that were the problem. They were untrue and had caused her to be sad, fearful, and delusional.

At the end of the week, I met with the counselor, psychiatrist, nurse, family doctor, and Julia before her release from the hospital. They diagnosed her with situational anxiety. I had never heard this term before, but I knew from what I witnessed with Julia that the diagnosis made sense. So they prescribed her low dosages of Zoloft, Clonazepam, and one other medication. She did begin to sleep better, and her anxiety lessened while on them.

But there was a downside: all the side effects. Her eyes were dilated all the time. She developed an increased appetite and couldn't tell when she was full. Therefore, she gained a lot of weight and even got up to 155 pounds. She is a 5-foot gal, so this was not good, especially since she couldn't walk and had to transfer herself for daily living needs.

But the worst part was, even though she wasn't my Julia when I brought her to the hospital, she *still* wasn't my Julia. It was as if a zombie had replaced my daughter. Her personality was gone or, at times, forced. She didn't feel like doing anything, though her Uncle Wayne would continue to pick her up to go out to eat or swim at the YMCA. Mentally, she couldn't think clearly and felt disoriented. She had no zeal for life and seemed to be in a numb state that lingered.

She rarely smiled. And neither did I.

The worst part was over — the crying and anxiety had stopped — which made life easier for both of us, but her soul had been stripped in the process. I hated the tradeoff and wanted my daughter back to how she used to be: fun-loving and sweet, a girl with a heart of gold.

"I consider that the sufferings we presently endure are not worth comparing with the glory to be revealed in us. Indeed, creation itself eagerly awaits the revelation of the children of God. For creation was subjected to frustration, not of its own choice but by the will of the one who subjected it, in the hope that creation itself will be freed from its slavery to corruption and share in the glorious freedom of the children of God."

(Romans 8:18-21)

CHAPTER 31

EVEN THOUGH JULIA'S DEMEANOR was different, she seemed to be better — we both did — and about a year passed in this way. I took a weekend to help move Emily and her husband from Branson, Missouri, to Dallas for a new city life.

Meanwhile, my relationship with my boyfriend was getting more serious, so much so that he invited me to move to his town an hour away. With the mental and emotional progress Julia had been making, there was really no reason for me to stay put. So, I accepted his invitation! And after some thought, I wondered if this might be the perfect time for Julia to live on her own. She was 25 years old, and it needed to happen sooner or later.

After Julia graduated high school, I had mulled over the idea of her finding her independence. Kathy had asked me over the phone a couple of times about what Julia would do after school and if I thought she should move into separate housing to start her own life. (She usually offered thought-provoking questions.) Julia needed to grow up and be on her own eventually, but I didn't believe she was mature enough and could not see myself letting go of her just yet.

But I knew Kathy was right, so I mentioned to Julia some positive reasons to move out on her own. "You could meet new people and make some friends," I coaxed.

"I can't and won't be here forever to help you, you know," I added. One day I said, "Let's go look at the apartments where you could stay." Julia didn't want anything to do with that and was adamant she wasn't even going to look. She was not interested. Nada. Nope. To her, her life was just fine, and this was one time I didn't prod her to make a decision she didn't want to do ... yet.

With my boyfriend and I moving in together and to a totally different town, I wondered if now was the time. I wasn't sure how Julia would react to the news, so I gave her a choice: to stay where we had been living or move with me. She chose not to go. I was so surprised! But it didn't take long after I left town — one short month later — for her to change her mind.

I sent her pictures of an apartment we found for her that was located across from the local community college. It was easily renovated for accessibility. I set her up in it before she arrived and also got the furniture ready and organized much of her clothes ahead of time to make it feel like home. The rest of her belongings moved on the day she did.

It was a rainy one. Thankfully, it didn't take us too many trips to get everything inside, but within five minutes of unpacking, my boyfriend said to me, "Okay, let's go!"

What? I thought. *This is too abrupt. It's too fast.* I looked at Julia. She looked at him and then back to me.

I didn't want to, but I hugged her and said goodbye. "I'll call you later," I promised.

As we left, the rain continued to fall. It felt like it was mirroring the turmoil and sadness in my heart. We would only be about 15 minutes away, but at that moment, it felt much farther.

For Julia, it was worse. She was surrounded by four new, strange walls and felt abandoned and alone. Her foundation had been ripped out from beneath her, and she missed her mom. She was more of a 15- or 16-year-old experientially who would be living on her own for the first time. I was worried she might make some decisions that she was not ready to make or wouldn't be the best for her or, worse, that she would relapse from the dark place we had worked so hard to get her out of.

Plus, I was with someone else, so she probably felt like she wasn't my number one priority anymore. But time progressed, I got married, and I wasn't as involved in her everyday life as I was in all the years prior. At one point, Julia sought out a counselor and asked me to join her for a session. It was pivotal for us, and we both broke down crying during it. While I wanted her to know how much I loved her but that it was time to create some separation for her to mature, it seemed as though this was her last ditch effort to take us back to what we were. It was so hard to see — what seemed to be — her figuratively flailing by herself, still wanting me around for stability and support. It felt like I had pushed her out of the nest with a broken wing.

Early on, my husband had decided I needed to "divorce" Julia, so to speak, so that we could live our lives and she could start building her own. He said I shouldn't call her, and if she called, I shouldn't pick up. To set boundaries, he said I should talk with her once a week, but that was it.

This was the complete opposite of who I was as a mom and everything I had done from the time Julia was born! But I wanted the marriage to work, and I did want Julia to make her own way in life like every other young adult, even if that meant she would make mistakes.

So I let go for a little while. And she did build her life.

With the help of the Center for Human Services, Julia found volunteer jobs. She graded kindergarten papers at a local school. Then she volunteered at a daycare and was even awarded Volunteer of the Year while there! She only quit volunteering at the daycare because of a timing conflict after she applied to attend and got into the local community college. The Boys and Girls Club, on the other hand, worked well with her school schedule. So her new routine became taking one class per semester and working about 15-18 hours a week.

Although the Boys and Girls Club just lasted two years due to a misunderstanding (it actually upset her a lot because she believed it was mostly due to her disability, and her job coach agreed), she continued her classes. But most importantly, she continued going to church.

About six months after Julia moved to her apartment, while riding the OATS transit bus to and from work, Julia's bus driver told her that he had to pick up another rider named Jason. After he got on, she could only see the back of his head since they were both in their wheelchairs, but there seemed to be a little matchmaking at play because the driver later asked Julia if he could share her phone number with Jason.

Being the outgoing person that she is and feeling maybe a little lonely yet excited that someone wanted to befriend her, Julia said sure, and before long, she and Jason became fast friends. He was an integral part of her mental and spiritual health changes, particularly because he introduced Julia to a nondenominational church called Liberty Life.

They went to many other churches together as well, including one that offered Celebrate Recovery meetings on Mondays for those overcoming trauma, which Julia attended. But the most important church in Julia's story has been Antioch Fellowship Church because it was the most impactful. She made friends with a couple, Debra and Jamie, who consistently picked her up for church on most Sundays and Wednesdays. They were like a family to her, very caring, kind, and always looking out for her. Jamie even told Julia that she didn't need to wait to be at service to ask for prayer, but that she could call them any time — morning, noon or night. And Julia said, "Mom, I know he meant it!" Through them and other people at Antioch, the Holy Spirit changed and saved her life.

There was one event during her spiritual awakening that was incredibly astonishing.

She told me on the phone that she would never forget what happened. It was a Friday morning. She was sitting in one of her aqua-colored recliners, curled up in a ball, her arms hugging her legs, when she suddenly saw an extra light in her house. It was brighter than any she had ever seen before coming through her window and front door.

At first, it scared her, but then she felt a presence inside her apartment, and the fear turned into a warm reassuring peace.

It was Jesus.

He asked her, "Are you ready to come home?" Somehow she knew what he meant. He continued, "Don't worry my child, I am here to save you, and fear not I am with you."

Julia was in awe. She felt as though her spiritual eyes had been unblinded, and she recognized who he was and the truth of everything He is.

And she knew that she believed. "Yes," Julia replied to His question. "I am ready to come home."

She said the light of Christ remained in her that day and has every day since. All she could do after the experience was reach for her Bible while playing worship songs in the background. It was like her heart knew what she needed before her mind could catch up. She began to recognize who she was in Christ, and every time she read the Bible, a song would play in tandem that would confirm what she was reading. Her elation grew and so did the feeling that her life was finally turning around.

She began attending Antioch even more regularly and making friends there. Antioch is a church that is big on prayer, so they prayed the spirit of suicide off her during one of the services. Later, she signed up for a Sozo, a kind of prayer and meditation session, with a few elders in the church. During it, the elders go to the root of the problem and seek to spiritually break off anything that is not of God. Julia had been under a spiritual attack for a long time, likely since her tween years, but after about two to three of these prayer times, she felt lighter, happier, and more back to herself.

This type of deliverance ministry seemed similar to Dr. Shipman's clearing prayers, which were also beneficial, so I understood the premise of it. I always believed Julia had a bright future, so, *of course, the darkness would want to take all of Julia's goodness away!* I was comforted by the fact that she was in great hands to deal with this at Antioch. More importantly, the Lord was taking care of her.

In fact, he seemed to be showering her with so much love and care that we began the process of reducing her prescription medications. Within just a year after her going to Antioch, she wasn't taking a single antidepressant, sleep aid, or anxiety medication. Some true healing had begun!

Hallelujah! Praise God!

Julia will tell you even today that God did this for her; she is so grateful! And afterward, the light had never shined so brightly from Julia. Of course, in the past, she had always been an inspiration to others because of her positive attitude, always attracted others to her and affected them in good ways. But this was different.

Many people noticed the change in Julia, me included. She had shared with me her "light" story after it happened, and I had wanted to believe her, especially because she explained it with so much enthusiasm. For a while I even told her, "I believe that you believe that."

You see, even though Julia is precious to me, she wasn't perfect. None of us are. For some years, she had been telling "tales" occasionally. Sometimes they were just exaggerated recollections of something that had happened; other times she would say things that I knew were false because she wanted me to drive her somewhere or because she just wanted me in general. I sternly told Julia: "You CAN NOT lie to me because should something truly happen, I wouldn't know if it was the truth or not!"

But she even pulled other people into the drama. One day Julia called 911 and told the person on the other end of the phone that she was losing weight and didn't feel good. An ambulance took her to the hospital, and I received a phone call from the counselor there who told me Julia was at the hospital because she was losing weight.

I said, "Does she look like she is losing weight?"

"No," the counselor admitted.

I replied, "The truth is that she is on pills and has been gaining weight. She is heavier than she's ever been."

She said, "Well, Julia wants you to pick her up with her van."

OH!!! That's when I realized she just wanted her van back and was also trying to find another way to see her mom. For some backstory, the van was to be used for Julia only, but I understood that she had been allowing other people to use it without her. I didn't want anything to happen to the van because it was for her benefit, so I stored it at my house.

"As difficult as this is for me," I told the counselor, "I have to show some tough love. I will not pick her up, and you can tell her she has to find her own way home."

Oh my gosh, this was SOOOOO HAAAAARD!!!

I added, "She knows how to call a cab." It felt so cold I could barely believe the words came out of my mouth.

But after being saved, things were different for Julia. I saw that she began posting on Facebook all about Jesus and daily sharing Bible verses. *Maybe this WAS a real Jesus encounter* ... Over time, she never quit, and it became harder to deny. I thought that if someone were to fib about something so big and supernatural, they likely would not be able to maintain the posts and overall joyful demeanor. I realized that she truly believed it, which meant I believed her and the Jesus encounter as well.

I especially wanted to know what her church, Antioch, was all about. How could I not? After all, this church and the people in it had helped Julia regain her sweet self, her personality, her soul. It also seemed so foreign to me, given my Catholic history. So I talked my husband into going one Sunday morning.

I was so moved by the Spirit while there that it brought tears to my eyes. I also witnessed Julia in church. She radiated something I hadn't seen in her before: pure, passionate praise. I knew somehow this place was a gift to my daughter and, in a roundabout way, to me, as well. There was more to come, I just didn't know it yet.

———*ele*———

"The Spirit and the Bride say, "Come." And let him who hears say, "Come." And let him who is thirsty come, let him who desires take the water of life without price."

(Revelation 17:22)

"He gives strength to the weary and increases the power of the weak."

(Isaiah 40:29)

CHAPTER 32

I HAD QUIT MY job when I married my second husband. He didn't want me to work, preferring I not be tied down if we wanted to go on a long weekend last minute. This made me feel a little aimless but also gave me the time to begin reading the Bible for the first time from cover to cover. (I was curious.) I also helped Emily and her husband move back to Missouri to our town and renovate their new house.

While Emily was in Dallas living the city life, she had found the country. She became fascinated with sustainability, preserving foods, organic farming, and gardening, which led to her to volunteer with a food co-op where members would pick up food that came from local farms. Through this she fell in love with the idea of having her own small farm. And I wanted to help her make it happen.

Coincidentally, there was a 3-acre farm not too far from us that was owned by my husband. It included a cute farmhouse that would require major renovations, but Emily and her husband decided to buy it. So while they were handing in their notices in Dallas, finding local jobs, and moving north, we began stripping the old hardwood floors, taking down paneling, painting, and even learning how to take down the old aeronautical map-themed wallpaper. My husband helped remove kitchen cabinets, paint doors and more.

Meanwhile, Emily designed her dream home renovation on grid paper like I had done so many times before. It was beautiful to see her light up when sharing her ideas with me. We then hired a contractor to finish what we couldn't. She was so proud of her home design, especially the kitchen, which was her favorite part, but she loved the green space with tall old trees and many flowering bushes too.

Emily and her husband moved in while the kitchen renovations were still underway, but they made do and started their farmette. They worked the farm around their jobs: in the mornings and evenings. Emily bought a miniature cow for milk. She had chickens first and then some ducks. She bought two barn cats, and others simply appeared. Lastly, they added a goldendoodle dog, Esme. She eventually planted a dwarf cherry tree, plum tree, and peach tree.

Her dream had come true!

Well, most of it. We both had hoped for more time together after she moved back, but that didn't happen, sadly. All three of us were busy, me with my husband, Emily with her husband, day job, and farm, and Julia with her schoolwork and boyfriend. Regretfully, we just didn't make time for it. However, it was comforting that both my girls were near me.

Julia was still seeing Jason. I wasn't aware of it initially, but the two of them would traipse all over town in their electric wheelchairs. One evening on our way to dinner, my husband and I were driving on Broadway Boulevard, which was typically a busy five-lane street.

"Oh my, WATCH OUT!" I cried. "There are some people driving their wheelchairs in the middle of the lane!" Since it was dusk, I couldn't make out who they were until we got closer, and when I did ...

"OH MY GOD!!" I exclaimed. "That's *Julia*! And *Jason*!"

I turned my head as far as I was able and watched them continue to roll down the highway with no orange flags, no reflectors, until they veered off onto a less-traveled street. I quickly dialed her number and, when she picked up, told her to "be careful" and "what are you doing going down a busy road?"

Julia later said, "The only thing that kept us safe that night was the light of Jesus Christ."

I had to give them a little grace with it all because I had wanted Julia to be independent, and the town was definitely not sidewalk friendly, especially not for wheelchair users. Plus cabs were rare and usually not accessible.

But still, she told me one day that she often chose to cross another 5-lane road and play Frogger, though "people slowed down for her." She giggled as she said it, not realizing that she had "told on" herself.

So after this and asking her many times to "not cross that street," Jason's mom helped them find some orange flags and reflectors, and I got some extra replacement batteries. She said the flag made her look like a dork and never attached it to her chair. However, Jason and Julia rarely used the streets again, to my knowledge at least, after that.

The two eventually had a difficult relationship. He proposed to her, and she said yes. I was shocked, to say the least, and went to her apartment to talk it through with her. "Can you imagine sitting at the table every meal with him forever?" I asked her. She admitted that even though Jason was a good person, her answer to that question and a few others I posed was definitely a "no." She knew she wasn't ready emotionally to get married either.

I wasn't the only one who was helping her think through the decision. She had a few mentors and friends who loved her, could speak into her life, and wanted her to make the right decision. *Thank God!* Julia was finding her independence alright, but she still wasn't mature enough to be married, and she didn't know how to stop what had started. She did not want the ring, so it was returned.

I knew this was really difficult for her. I was sad she and Jason hadn't worked out too but was grateful that he and Julia met because I believed it was in God's plan for her testimony to proceed the way it did. God brought Jason into her life so that she found the church that prayed for her, and he encouraged her to attend church with all the people who were instrumental in her spiritual and emotional growth.

I could see how God was working in Julia's life and wondered, *Will He do it in mine too?*

"In their hearts humans plan their course, but the Lord establishes their steps."
(Proverbs 16:9)

CHAPTER 33

By 2019, MY SECOND marriage was declining. I never thought I would have one divorce, much less two, but after just four years, I needed to find a new place to live and income. Massage came back to mind.

Prior to my second marriage, I had continued to extend my massage therapy license even though I was no longer running a business. I knew the process to reinstate it would be difficult. But when my husband asked me not to work, and especially didn't want me giving massages, I let it expire.

Now, years later, I wanted it back. To get my license again, I had to go through the full reinstatement process, filling out pages of paperwork for the Missouri state government. So I did.

I found a part-time massage position with a local spa. The gals there were supportive, but after being there for a month, I decided to move on because the percentage the spa was taking from my business, though reasonable, was too much; there wasn't enough left for me to pay all of my bills.

After that I experienced obstacle after obstacle as I sought to grow my own massage business. But I didn't give up.

I set up a location with a chiropractor first. The picture in my office said, "You will be blessed when you come in and blessed when you go out," Deuteronomy 28:6, which was my mission.

Then I moved on to a small room in the back of a health food store. I had bought all my supplies over the weekend and was expecting to move in that Monday, but surprisingly, due to mistakenly missing a clause in the rental contract, it was deemed I couldn't practice there.

Next, a kind massage therapist allowed me to use her office only if I gave her massages as rent. I did this briefly until I asked Julia if I could offer massages at her apartment for just three months while I was waiting for my house to be completed.

"I'm not going to tell you no, Mom," she replied.

I had been living at her apartment since my husband and I separated. Originally, I was a little nervous about moving in with her because I didn't want her to cling instead of continuing to grow into her independence. However, I began going to Antioch with her regularly, which was one way we spent quality time together.

After six months, which was longer than I had anticipated, I was able to move out, and I'll never forget what she said when I told her the news ... "THANK GOD!" Her tone was full of enthusiasm and relief. At this, we both laughed out loud because, honestly, I was thinking the same thing.

I often joked throughout the years that Julia and I were attached by the umbilical cord and we didn't know how to let go.

Was it me who was holding on?

Was it her who thought she needed to be with me so I wouldn't be alone, or did she not want to grow up?

It might have been all three. I don't know.

But again, *THANK GOD!* We had done it!

We were able to let go of the tight tie that bound us... for the most part.

There were a couple big positives that had resulted from my second marriage. One was that it had given me time to read the Bible cover to cover— something I always wanted to do.

Second—and maybe even more impactful—was that if God hadn't brought my second husband into my life, I likely never would have encouraged Julia to move out on her own. I would have continued feeling responsible for her, and she likely would have clung to me in a way that wasn't healthy for either of us. Honestly, we might have ended up living together for the rest of our lives.

Coincidentally, Julia had moved in next door to a mom and daughter who were 80 and 55. Their situation was very different from ours, but God still showed me what could have been our future reality if He hadn't taken the reins and separated us.

This didn't mean I was done trying to help improve her life, though. We began to take road trips together again. Once, when we were on our way back from an appointment with Dr. Shipman in Arkansas, there was a horrible storm showing blackish green clouds rolling behind us, lightning, thunder, with a tornado threat chasing us north.

By the time we arrived in Lincoln, Missouri, it had caught up to us. We parked under a gas station overhang when it became too intense to drive in. It was pouring, lightning and thunder lit the sky, and the wind was rocking the van.

Amid the chaos, Julia made her typical announcement, "I have to go to the bathroom. Badly!"

My eyes rolled, and I sighed. "Really?" Then I answered my own question, exasperated yet with a chuckle. "Of course you do!"

We checked the Doppler radar to see if we'd get any relief from the storm in order to make it home for Julia to go to the bathroom. No luck. The clouds were only building.

The lights were off inside the station where we had parked — I thought they were smart to close and go home early — but there was another station open across the narrow city street. I noticed cars were driving across water that looked to be 18 inches deep and knew there was no way I could get our lowered van through it or roll Julia through it safely. Plus, the storm was relentless!

So I succumbed to the inevitable and squeezed my way through the front bucket seats to search for the plastic seat cover that always fell off the driver's seat.

Chuckling and holding it up like a trophy, I asked, "How about going in this?"

"That isn't going to work!" she said, already envisioning disaster.

"Well, go in this or don't go," I retorted. "I have nothing else!"

We both had visions of her balancing outside the passenger's front door and going in the rain and knew it wasn't going to work. So, for the next few minutes, I prepared the back of the van before assisting Julia as she wedged herself between the seats to get to her wheelchair, which made her have to go even more. She sat in the wheelchair, and I arranged the plastic piece where I thought would be best so she could stand up to go. It all seemed absurd, and we couldn't help but giggle through this whole process.

"Don't make me laugh!" Julia cried. "I can't hold it any longer!" But this made us both burst with laughter all the more.

We finally managed to get her up so she could go, and as the rain poured outside, the pee began to fall inside. We both said, "Dear God, please let it fall where it should," not wanting a repeat of the snowy 1998 accident.

And thank goodness, it did!

Afterward, I helped Julia back into her chair, both of us still laughing, and then opened the side door to dump out the plastic piece, hoping the wind was blowing the other way to avoid some backsplash. I quickly closed the door and wiped the plastic out with restaurant napkins that had been left in the van for such a time as this. (Not!) We waited out the storm for a bit before heading out again and hoping our next trip to Arkansas wouldn't be as eventful.

Not too long after that, Dr. Shipman called us out of the blue to share a new modality. You see, God had given him visions of Julia walking in his church years ago. He did not want to give up on her miracle either and consistently prayed for her healing, whether an earthly one or a supernatural one. Dr. Shipman usually ended his phone calls with us by saying, "Julia, you have a heart of gold."

Julia and I had not gone to any treatments for over seven years; instead, she had received massages from different therapists, including me. After researching Neufit's website, I found it explained the device and treatment like this:

The Neubie device (Neuro-Bio-Electric-Stimulator) is a groundbreaking approach to rehabilitation and performance enhancement. Using direct current to offer targeted stimulation, the Neubie promotes faster healing, pain reduction, and strength improvements.

The process begins with a comprehensive body mapping to pinpoint the areas where the nervous system is restricting movement and muscle function. Practitioners apply electricity-conducting pads along nerve pathways to detect these limitations, often feeling intensely sensitive to the patient like a trigger point.

After identifying limiting patterns, they reset them using manual muscle activation techniques, targeted electrical stimulation, and specific exercises. This process recalibrates the nervous system, adjusting overprotective reflexes to appropriate levels without eliminating necessary self-protection mechanisms.

When Julia was young, thirty years ago, a friend once reminded me that technology continues to evolve and you never know what might be invented that could help children with disabilities. Well, this statement continued to prove true. So after we discovered that a gentleman in northwest Arkansas had a Neubie device, we traveled there to try it.

Sixth Alternative Treatment: E-Stim Therapy through the Neubie Device

Julia went through the entire process in addition to a protocol for relaxation. The whole time, she was in control of the intensity, telling the practitioner when to increase or decrease it. I was in the room and watched how it all was administered throughout the treatment.

Julia felt some benefits from the therapy; it relaxed her back, hips, and legs so she could sit better in her wheelchair. It would be very useful, especially for Julia, for any strains, sprains, and joint issues and could also calm the vagus nerve. It also increased her strength and range of motion in her upper legs some.

However, while researching more about this treatment on a Facebook page, I noticed that other practitioners were posting about Frequency Specific Microcurrent (FSM) therapy. FSM therapy is a treatment system that uses very low direct electrical currents, known as micro amperage, to promote healing. By applying specific hz frequencies to the body, you can address various conditions, particularly muscle regulation and nerve pain, inflammation, scar tissue, and more. It's typically painless.

Wow! I thought. *Where has this been?*

Interestingly enough, FSM therapy has been around since the 1920s. Carol McMakin's book, *The Resonance Effect*, explains a lot about its history and uses. I read this book and, in February 2022, traveled to Arizona to attend the CORE seminar and learn more about this type of therapy. I felt like I did when I went to Futures Unlimited for the first time. That this could be a great benefit for Julia.

While there, I had a brief visit with Dr. McMakin and asked her some questions about how FSM therapy could help adults with cerebral palsy like my daughter. The first thing she asked me was: "Does she want to do this?"

That thought hadn't even crossed my mind. *Why would she not?* I asked myself rhetorically. But it did cause me to pause before answering. "I assume so."

After returning home, I searched for FSM practitioners, and about three chiropractors lived within a day's travel from us. I left messages with all three, but only one called back: Dr. Leslie Churchill. She was incredibly honest about FSM, very kind, and took her time over the phone, so we made an appointment to see her in Omaha, Nebraska.

Seventh Alternative Treatment: Frequency Specific Microcurrent Therapy

Over the course of three days, though the treatment was only a couple hours each day, Julia received FSM therapy. And when a "pair" of frequencies would positively affect her, she got the "dude" feeling, or drowsy. Other positive effects were an improved attention span and better sleep. While we were there, Dr. Churchill also gave Julia a chiropractic adjustment, which took care of the headaches Julia had experienced off and on for many years. She even texted me to see how Julia was doing after the sessions. Needless to say, we returned home with a new special friend in Dr. Churchill.

I decided to purchase an FSM device because it just made sense to use our money in this way rather than for travel costs. The machine is much smaller than the Neubie device, and it gives a very low intensity that is not felt at all. There are many ways to give the treatment, including the use of alligator clips to attach the leads from the wet towels to the device, which is the process I usually chose for Julia. After I took a basic FSM class, we mostly used it for her sore muscles after swimming. It reduced Julia's soreness to almost nothing; usually she would have delayed onset muscle soreness for two days.

Eventually, I wanted to know more, so the following year I went to an advanced FSM class. Like the first class, I attended it with our friend Judy who we met while attending MFR treatments in Sedona. It was nice to have a friend there with me to bounce ideas off and just simply for memory. There was so much to learn! While at the advanced class, a few doctors who treat cerebral palsy patients were there, and I was fortunate enough that they spent a little time answering my questions during a break.

When we returned home, Julia tried one that was supposed to help her improve her attention span and brain fog. She attended only one college class a semester because it took her a while to finish homework, and after utilizing that one protocol, Julia said she was able to finish her homework much quicker. She received the protocol a couple more times, which has allowed her to retain and comprehend what she reads more easily, so it was a huge win for her mentality. But after that, she rarely asked to use the FSM device except for soreness.

During my first FSM class, I had also learned about an optometrist who had a technique to help with lazy eye. If it worked, Julia might be able to drive! We called the doctor who said we needed to find an old TV that could be paired with 3D glasses. Then Julia could use them to watch Disney movies to help her eyes converge. I tried to help Julia find these items but eventually told her to continue searching if she wanted to drive.

She never did. Yes, she was busy with school, but I felt there was something deeper going on. One day, I asked her about it. "Why aren't you using these devices or searching for the TV? Do you forget? Or are you afraid to walk?"

Her reply was, "No, but yes. If I could walk, my life would be different!"

"Yes, you would be free to go and do whenever and wherever you wanted. But along with that, you would be responsible for yourself." Then I added, "But the freedom outweighs the responsibility."

She was quiet after that. And that was okay.

Even though Julia had shared with me that she had dreamed of having a different life, I knew there was a comfort in familiar...and a fear of the unknown. But, it was at this moment that I was finally able to recognize her as an adult who could and should make her own choices. And all I had to do was let her.

"And my God will supply every need of yours according to his riches in glory in Christ Jesus." (Philippians 4:19)

CHAPTER 34

GOD WAS BEGINNING TO work on my heart. I could not get enough of the Bible. The music in my car switched to worship almost all the time, and I listened to many pastors online to learn more. Not only was I going with Julia to the Sunday service and Wednesday teachings at Antioch, but I was also still volunteering at the Sacred Heart Catholic Church by opening up the Adoration Chapel so that others could pray.

This was something I had done for about five years, and even though I attended Antioch, I felt I should continue serving in this way at Sacred Heart. Plus it was an important part of my week because I would use the time to pray and just be with Him. I loved to sing to Him too if nobody else was in the chapel.

Dr. Shipman and his wife, Rebbecca, also invited Julia and me to go to The Rock of Northwest Arkansas church one weekend because there was going to be a guest speaker. They were the most caring, welcoming, and servant-hearted couple, and we had become friends through the years in addition to being clients. Rebbecca typically invited us to stay at their home.

We enjoyed our visits with them both and even went to one or two gatherings. One was for a church Christmas party and another a church anniversary. But for some reason, this time Julia didn't want to go and told me to "have a nice trip by yourself." I was in disbelief, but knew it would still be a good weekend. *Who knows what the Holy Spirit has in store!*

During the service, an evangelist from Oklahoma was introduced. I can't remember her name, but I do remember she was an attractive person with very dark brown hair, and that there was something special about her. When I saw her, she was simply full of love. It exuded from her eyes.

I thought, *Wow, how can I have that?*

She began telling her story of how she got to where she loved Christ and how he brought her to this point of helping people come to Christ. The longer she talked, the more her hands started to shake. She explained that when the Holy Spirit starts to take over, sometimes this is what happens. It was difficult to ignore yet intriguing. Then, at the end of her talk, she asked: "Who here has an overbearing mother?"

That question hit home with me. Suddenly everything significant I remember my mother telling me at different times in my life was flashing through my mind.

Now, about my Mom. I love her dearly, as I did my dad. She was incredibly hard working, and with her get-it-done attitude, she could do anything. And did. Not only did she raise four children, but she also ran the business side of the farm while gardening, canning, sewing our clothes, doing upholstery work, cleaning houses, picking berries and freezing them, baking and selling bread at the farmers market. She was an angel to my dad over the course of their 57 years together. He had experienced heart problems that sent him to the hospital multiple times, and she stayed by his side devotedly until 2014 when he went to see the Lord.

I always knew my mom loved me. She loved all her children, and as our mother, only wanted to protect us and wished the best for us. And when I was young,

I had always thought my mom was overprotective because of the incidents that happened in her life. However, the older I got, the more I felt that she was overbearing and controlling; perhaps she was finding it hard to let go of us kids.

I realized that I had grown used to listening to what my mom told me rather than doing and following my own processing. It gave me a skewed perspective of myself and made things difficult for me when making decisions, especially if I had her voice in my head saying, "Why would you do that?" or "You can't do that."

While I had forgiven my mom years prior, if anything should have been forgiven, at this time, I still felt the heaviness. And it had weighed on me and likely affected every area of my life.

"If this is you," the evangelist added, "Come forward to the front."

I was the first to move.

Now, I don't have a personality that wants to be in front of people, but I couldn't stop myself from walking forward. It was as if I felt a "hand" on my back nudging me to go. My heart was beating quickly, strongly — the Holy Spirit was drawing me in. Although I didn't know what to expect, I was standing there ready to accept whatever He was going to do for me.

When I reached the evangelist, there were already tears in my eyes and I was shaking on the inside. First, she prayed for me and my relationship with my mom. It was incredible because all her words from the Holy Spirit were correct and exactly what I needed to hear. She then asked me if I wanted to accept Jesus as my Savior and ask the Holy Spirit into my heart. I told her I did, and she quietly took me through some questions to answer while touching my heart with her hand.

Suddenly my right arm went up to touch "heaven." It was as if His fire was being transferred to me. My arm started to shake, and my whole body felt like I was in another place. I kept standing there shaking, my arm and my body swaying, my eyes closed. And when her hand left my heart, I could feel that the Holy Spirit was still there.

As the evangelist moved on to pray for another person who had come to the front, I spent a brief time reaching up for Him with my arm. When I opened my eyes next, the evangelist was looking back at me, and I knew the gaze was spirit to spirit. Then she walked back to me, gently touched me again, and I fell backward onto the floor... the spirit language bursting out of my mouth!

What is coming out of my mouth?! I thought in awe. *And what just happened to me?*

I am typically NOT outspoken, but there I was speaking in the spirit language. And it was loud!

I had never felt this way in my whole life and continued praising in tongues for a while, lying on the floor of the church, my body shaking with my arm still above me. Briefly, I remembered having a MFR session during which I released emotions, but this was entirely different! It could not be compared. It was supernatural, holy.

As the shaking began to cease and my Spirit language faded, I started looking around and realized more people were falling in the Spirit. I glanced back at Dr. Shipman and his wife, Rebbecca, who had never failed to spiritually strengthen and encourage me.

Simultaneously, Dr. Shipman said, "Finally!"

Rebbecca exclaimed, "Praise God!"

I lay there, filled with gratitude, praise, and honoring God in my mind by thanking Jesus. Then I giggled with joy while the tears continued to flow.

Eventually, I decided I should go back to my seat because others needed the floor space. I sat there in a daze but with a lightness inside me I had never known before. One congregant walked over and said to me, "Don't go back to where you were before." It was such a prophetic statement for me. I knew what that meant. To stay in the Spirit. Walk in the Spirit. Be one with the Spirit.

After this encounter, I discovered that I wasn't in such a hurry. There was a greater settling inside me — a peace. I began to learn how to be closer to Him, and He moved me to the most profound gratitude in my heart, knowing this path was His plan.

Later Rebbecca mentioned she wished Julia would have come to the service too. But it was clear to me why Julia chose not to. Usually, if Julia is with me, I take the "backseat." She receives the attention, and I let her shine. I explained this to Rebbecca. "I know if she had come along, I likely would not have walked forward because I would have still been too focused on her."

Our children, without even realizing it, are sometimes the mirror to ourselves, our teachers, our heroes. What we do in relation to them can bring forth both positive and negative attributes, showing us where we need to grow.

The absence of Julia allowed one of the most important events of my life to transpire. But it wasn't because she was at fault whenever we were together; I just needed to finally give myself the freedom to do something for myself. To see God!

My eyes had been opened to the truth, to God's love, and to the Savior who carries our burdens. *Thank you, Jesus!*

"For this reason I remind you to fan into flame the gift of God, which is in you through the laying on of my hands." (2 Timothy 1:6)

"For the Lord God is brighter than the brilliance of a sunrise! Wrapping himself around me like a shield, he is so generous with his gifts of grace and glory. Those who walk along his paths with integrity will never lack one thing they need, for he provides it all!" (Psalm 84:11)

Chapter 35

After my encounter in Arkansas, I was filled with joy, even more grateful for my blessings, and had a greater spiritual fervor than ever before! That doesn't mean that things were easy, though. Allow me to let you in on the reality of being a believer: even though I love Him, living one with the spirit was and is a constant challenge.

But every day I found myself getting better emotionally, mentally and spiritually. I continued to read my Bible, and Julia and I even started reading healing scriptures together.

At Antioch, my home church, I began to feel more tugging at my heart. One night I had a dream that continued to be extremely vivid — unforgettable.

I was standing on the edge of a very tall silo with unusual water inside when, suddenly, the silo water started to swell. It grew so large that it turned into a huge bright aqua-blue wave that overcame me. Strangely, I wasn't scared. As it overtook me, I fell from the rim of the silo and onto the wave's white foam, and it held me up like a soft pillow or cloud.

When I woke up, I knew I should be baptized again!

Our pastor announced that they would be having baptisms in a couple of weeks, so I signed up. Possibly being baptized in the Spirit first and then water is a little backward, but this is how it all happened for me.

Years ago, Emily had asked me to watch her be baptized in a Baptist church when she was in high school and active with Young LIfe. I asked her, "You've already been baptized. Why do it again?" She tried to explain that it was her personal choice and a declaration of her faith, but I still didn't fully understand this due to my Catholic mentality.

But I went, of course, and was happy for her. Now, years later, I understood what she had been saying. I was so full of joy, so overwhelmed with love for God, that I wanted to be baptized again. Not because my first didn't matter, but because this one came from a place of personal encounter and deep conviction.

Before my second baptism, I shared my dream with the congregation and felt a bit overwhelmed before going under, anticipating a new life in Christ. Allowing everything in my past to be washed away was invigorating; I felt even more full of gratitude for the peace that surrounded me.

Not too long after my baptism, I also began serving in the church by singing with the praise and worship team. In the past, I had always sat toward the back of the church just like I did when attending Catholic Mass. I loved to sing, so I didn't care who heard me worship from my heart, and sometimes I felt a subtle pull that made me wonder if I should be praising Jesus at the front of the sanctuary.

One Sunday, a friend, Stacy, prophesied that someone in the church should be singing with the praise and worship team. This resonated with me. There had always been a love for it, but I was never sure if my gift would simply be something I did at home or if it would extend outward to others.

As I said, God was tugging at my heart. Soon after this prophecy, I felt a greater urge and mentioned to Pastor Steve and his wife, Ann, that, if they were willing, I would try to sing with the praise and worship team.

Pastor Steve and Debra, met me at the church one day to hear my voice, and after singing a few songs, he asked, "When do you want to start?"

The next Sunday I was a bit shy in my singing and kept the microphone too far away from my lips, especially because I was learning new songs. After a few months, though, I found my rhythm and was comfortable enough to sing. I worshipped my heart out to God and helped others feel His presence, too.

My life wasn't only changing at church either. For one, my massage business was growing!

It was the beginning of 2020 when I moved to my small but comfortable new home after the divorce and set up a treatment room in my third bedroom. I worked for about four weeks, which was long enough to get my feet wet.

Then our state locked everyone down.

This turned into a six-week waiting period for me, and after having taken a break from massage some years ago, I worried what might become of my business. It all felt like the twilight zone for not only my business but also the entire world.

To pass the time during the lockdown, I worked on my home, setting up my yard landscaping, garden and home decor. It felt good to organize and create in the middle of so much global chaos.

I also tried a new hobby: painting. My brother Don had helped me chainsaw some of the better boards from a warped and weatherworn chicken shed at the farm. I cleaned them and then covered them with an acrylic glaze. These oak boards worked perfectly to paint landscapes, which usually included a church with Holy Spirit fire bursting out from within. Each painting also included a Bible verse that was inspired by the painting.

Surprisingly, I sold a few at a shop, Handel Haus, in Cole Camp, a small German town nearby. This was only for a season, but it was an enlightening and joyous one, and I discovered I had more of a creative side than I imagined.

Eventually, I was able to call my clients and tell them that if they had no symptoms, I could see them if they were willing to see me. Most of them were happy to get back to their treatments because it had been a while and they needed pain relief. In my opinion, massage was medically necessary for some clients; additionally, everyone had been isolated, which meant that many people needed physical touch, even if it was from a therapeutic massage.

My clientele was fantastic, and the number of clients began to steadily grow. It made me especially happy to hear that they had truly been helped and massage had relieved their pain. I thanked God for being with me during my treatments and propelling me to do this work in the first place. I've always heard that when you go to work, make sure you love what you do—- and I absolutely love what I do! I felt like I had finally walked into my purpose in life — well, outside of raising my daughters — after waiting for so many years.

Another dream was coming true at this time too. Not only were Emily and Julia visiting more and going to movies together, but Emily was also beginning to come to my house once a week to talk and was going to lunch with me more often on some weekends. She would even purchase tickets to musicals and invite me to go, and I planned shopping sprees with her to our favorite store where we would spend hours trying on clothes.

One time, Emily and I were meeting Julia at her apartment. My slippers are so comfortable that I forgot to change into my shoes before we drove there. However, I didn't realize it until I got out of the vehicle and looked down. I started laughing and pointed at my feet to Emily. She looked down and began to laugh too! I couldn't remember the last time we had laughed together like that.

These small moments were big moments for me — glimmers of hope as Emily and I were getting to know each other again. She was always such a precious gift to me, but over the years it seemed we were being moved by opposing forces. There were times when I just couldn't say anything right or she was very short with me. I knew it was because she might have been lamenting her life growing up, so I let her be.

Recently, Julia, Emily and I all went to the wedding of my goddaughter Mackenzie and her now husband, Blake. We were walking into the church (well, Julia was rolling), and one of our friends came toward us on the opposite sidewalk. She said "hello" but only looked at Julia. Emily and I said hello back, but it quickly became clear the conversation was solely with Julia.

This was typical, but as Emily and I walked into church, I looked at her and said jokingly, "How does it feel to be invisible?"

"Just like my whole life!" she replied.

I told her I understood, and though it broke my heart to hear her say it, I think this is in some odd way, a bond we share.

Julia had heard what we said and later whispered, "I can't help it."

"I know, Julia," I whispered back. "Don't worry about it! It isn't your fault."

And it isn't. In fact, it's nobody's fault. It's a blessing she is so loved and is a blessing to others in return. I never minded being in her shadow, but now, even more so, I feel as though her light is her gift, and I love to see her shine.

Another day, while I was visiting Emily at her home and helping her pick and pit the cherries, I felt a nudge to speak from my heart. I told her I was sorry. Sorry for anything I said or didn't say, do or didn't do for or with her over the years.

She very lovingly said through the branches of the cherry tree, "Mom, it wasn't like that, and none of what has happened is your fault. It was just the situation. And I don't regret my childhood; it made me who I am today."

She added: "We all do the best we can with what we have."

My heart melted and quietly began crying. It was a rare moment for both of us. No further words were needed.

Over the years, we have both softened. Emily has been to counseling, and I am so proud of the courage she's shown in doing that. We've both learned to listen with more grace. We don't always agree and sometimes we agree to disagree about certain subjects. For example, now that I've made the switch from Catholicism to non denominational, she's stepped away from religion in general to her own form of spirituality — but we love each other despite those instances. We respect each other too, knowing it is our own journey, and have even learned to forgive. I know God sees Emily, and I continue to pray for her.

Emily began to share the concerns she has about her future like career moves and relationships, and this made me feel so loved because she trusted me enough to confide in me at times. In turn, I told her the concerns about my own life. She's such an active listener and always knows exactly what to say. This has bonded us even more as we've both gone through career moves, divorce, spiritual shifts, and lifestyle changes. Now most weeks we share the good and bad with each other, but best of all, we share those long hugs that are healing for both of us.

I thank God every day that I feel closer than ever with my oldest daughter. It is such a blessing to hear Emily say some of my favorite and most endearing words as she leaves my home: "Love you, Momma!"

"Love is patient, love is kind. It does not envy, it does not boast, it is not proud. It does not dishonor others, it is not self-seeking, it is not easily angered, it keeps no record of wrongs. Love does not delight in evil but rejoices with the truth. It always protects, always trusts, always hopes, always perseveres." (1 Corinthians 13:4-7)

CHAPTER 36

A GOOD FRIEND FROM church, Apostle Harvey, kindly said after he had gotten to know Julia and me: "Marilyn, you need to slow down. And Julia, you need to speed up!" And he was right! *I typically walk fast, and she rolls slowly*, I thought with a chuckle.

For so many years, I felt like it was my duty — my calling, even — and responsibility as a mom to set aside my own needs and desires to help Julia. When she was younger, the responsibility was a given. But as she grew older, that "habit" of taking care of her and ultimately trying to help her walk never left me. It was my goal for her to live in this world as easily as possible — to be healed.

So, we went from one (earthly) therapy or healing modality to the next and the next and the next, my hope remaining steadfast with every small benefit she received from them. But these treatments never truly helped her walk.

Still, I clung to the hope, sometimes out of faith and sometimes out of sheer determination. I believed that if we just found the *right* therapy, the *right* specialist, the *right* breakthrough, she would rise up and walk. It was as if my heart couldn't let go of that vision. Maybe because letting go of it felt like giving up. And giving up was never an option for me as her mother.

And yet, Julia is a miracle! She flailed between life and death twice as a newborn, but God was insistent that she live. I've often wondered if God had a conversation with her each time it happened, telling her it wasn't time, and to go back and "do my work." As a young adult, it was Julia's spirit that diminished, but God brought her back again! And with more fullness and wholeness than I could have ever imagined.

Her journey may not have followed the path I once envisioned, but it has been divinely woven in its own way — beautiful, intricate, and filled with quiet strength. God didn't heal her legs, but He healed so much more. He restored her spirit. And watching her light shine from a place of deep inner peace has been its own kind of miracle, one that reminds me every day that healing comes in many forms.

I had heard people tell their stories about how God or Jesus presented Himself to them. I never imagined that someone I knew would have that supernatural experience. But He did the ultimate act — for *my* daughter! God revealed Himself to Julia, and she accepted His free gift of salvation.

Since then she has made it her mission to help others find spiritual healing, and in turn, emotional and physical healing. And her passion is palpable! She rarely fails to post a daily inspirational message and consistently prays for her family and friends and even the strangers she meets or has never met.

When I look at Julia's life, I'm blown away by her. She has God's strength and is an overcomer, and she has a purpose and is living in her purpose. Others see her as an inspiration; most don't even notice her chair. If you have a child with special needs and sometimes the world deems them imperfect, please know that they are perfect to God. And that's truly the only thing that matters. You can see the light in these children's eyes, and it is God's light showing us the way to His love.

Remember the memory I shared at the beginning of this book about crying at Mary's feet? I now believe that somehow God was already showing my soul that my journey as a mother would often be wonderful, but difficult. Perhaps I was even unknowingly grieving the future sacrifices and decisions I would need to make for my daughters. Not to mention the sacrifices they would make and struggles they would face because of those choices.

I was often angry at God for giving us this life, especially during the times I felt so alone while working so hard or when Julia had her dark valleys or Emily questioned whether she truly mattered. There are moments when I still ponder: *Why did we have to struggle so much? Did Julia really have to have cerebral palsy for us to find spiritual healing?*

But the journey has always been worth it, and I know — without a doubt — God has been with all three of us every step of the way. Even 50 years ago while I was looking up at the comforting face of Mary, God was already writing my story. He knew I would be a mom to two beautiful girls. He knew that they would be my greatest joys and most treasured blessings. And He knew they would help lead me to the ultimate healing of my soul through Christ's salvation.

HE KNEW!

I've often wondered what I was truly searching for. Was it only Julia's healing? Or, was I, in part, seeking my own? For so long, I was her compass, guiding her every "step." But over time, in ways I never expected, she became a compass for me, leading with grace, resilience, and a light that has helped guide my own healing path.

Now I know that the ups and downs I've experienced — the curves in the road and the straightaways, the storms and the pleasant sceneries, the setbacks and the victories, the laughter and the tears, the light and the darkness, the pleading and the praising, the physical moves and the spiritual revelations — were all drawing me closer to one thing: the deep, abiding love of Jesus.

And it's within that love that I have learned to embrace myself for who I am but more who He created me to be, to let go of the pain I've experienced from life's hardships, to be thankful for the richness he has bestowed upon my life, and to become an even better mom than I was before. It isn't about what He can do for our lives; it's about what we can do for Him.

That doesn't mean I'm done hoping for the hand of God to heal Julia. I still believe He can. I've just come to understand, in retrospect, that the continuous seeking of possible healing modalities, desperate prayers, and the letting go, were not just about finding a cure. It was about God urging me to throw up my hands and allow Julia to mature in her own way, which brought us closer to our One True Healer, Jesus Christ.

He may not decide to heal Julia on this side of heaven, and if that's the case, then another healing is in her future.

"I'll be dancing in heaven!" Julia tells me, and I know there's no doubt about it.

But because of the healing He's done in my own life, I also believe that He can work miracles, and if He wants to provide total restoration for Julia on this earth, He absolutely can — and will. So many caretakers, practitioners, therapists, friends, and pastors, and prophets have shared with Julia and me that they have had visions or dreams of her walking.

Yes, yes, yes! Lord, let's do this! And if it happens, "God, You will receive all the glory."

Until then, I will continue to hope and prayerfully, and humbly, yet confidently ask Him:

Will you do it, Lord?

"Now to Him who is able to do immeasurably more than all we ask or imagine, according to His power that is at work within us..."

(*Ephesians 3:20*)

Epilogue

SUMMER OF 2024, JULIA called one morning as usual. "Mom, I want to tell you about the dream I had last night." There was urgency and excitement in her voice.

She said she was inside the sanctuary of our church. Emily and I were also in the room. The colors surrounding her were bright and vivid, Julia noted. Suddenly, Dolly Morris, a woman from Antioch who had guided Julia when I was not around as much, handed her a letter.

It was from ... me.

When she opened it, there was just one sentence written there: *Now go and give God all the Glory. — Love, Mom*

Julia and I weren't exactly sure what the dream meant. Was it simply an assurance for Julia that her mission is to bring God glory or an even greater message that she will have the opportunity to change the world through her experiences and joy? For me, was it a dream through Julia in which God was showing that He was proud of all that I had done for both of my daughters? Or confirmation that the work was "done" and that it is (finally) time for me to hand them over to Him, stand back, and proudly watch my girls live their lives?

All Julia and I know is that the dream touched us deeply, especially because when Julia was receiving the letter, she wasn't looking up at us from her chair.

In the dream, she was standing!!!

Hallelujah!

"Very soon you will smile and say, God, this is more than I prayed for."

(Philippians 4:19)

I PRAY OUR STORY was encouraging to you, so much so that you want to be closer to Jesus Christ, our Lord and Savior.

If you are drawn to repent of your sins, meaning you feel sorry for them and want to turn away from them to do them no more, and believe in your heart that God sent His only Son, Jesus, to die on the cross to cover our sins so that we are saved from eternal death and can now have eternal life, I encourage you to do just that. Repent and profess your belief.

I also urge you to find a church to experience baptism in water and the fire of the Holy Spirit.

All Glory be to God, always!

Acknowledgments

I AM SO GRATEFUL for everyone who has been a part of my life story, and I can see now how many people subtly, and sometimes not so subtly, were gifted to me by God. Some of the most significant people in our lives were all of Julia's amazing teachers, aides, and therapists who met us with love, took a special interest in Julia's needs (and mine), and dedicated their lives to the healing of others. Although, unfortunately, every person who has had a positive impact on my life was not included in this memoir, all of you were and are profoundly important to my soul. From the bottom of my heart, thank you.

More specifically, thanks to ...

God, to whom I give all the Glory for my life, for his love, strength, and support throughout the years, mostly at times when I didn't even know or believe He was there. He provided a host of angels that came to my rescue when I didn't know I needed rescuing. And, He gifted me my daughters who have given me insight not only into myself but also into the world around me. Through them, He has shown me what unconditional love is.

Emily Long, for always challenging me and opening my eyes to new experiences. You are one of the most caring, loving, and forgiving people I think I've ever known, and you will make a wonderful counselor someday. You are full of beautiful gifts from God, and I am so blessed that you are my daughter and I am able to call you my friend. Thank you for asking for my help and allowing me to support you, and I pray that God's purpose will manifest in you soon. Also, for reviewing my book, remembering the parts I didn't, and allowing me to share some of your perspective. You had your own journey through all of this, and if this book was solely about you, it would have been titled, "What about me!?" You are the most amazing gift, and I cherish you. I love you, even more today because of how we have grown together. You are my first sunshine!

Julia Lehman, for the adventure God took us on, even if it was by my leading at times. It was one of healing, and it was more than I ever dreamed it would be — the laughter, experiences, and most importantly, the love. Also, for all the hours listening to me read so many stories to ensure they aligned with your memories as well. You are a trooper in life; you watched me going through all my struggles, even outside of the ones related to you, yet you remained steadfast through them all. Watching you grow in the Lord has been another miracle and an inspiration to me! It is obvious that I love you, but just know that through this wild ride you were the catalyst from which my love grew for God. Deep gratitude will never encompass or explain fully how I feel about your part in my life. Keep doing what you do best: spreading love, prayer, praise, and sunshine!

Kathy Eggen, for a lifetime of love and support, and for stepping in as one of my alpha readers. Your willingness to walk alongside me in this process means more than I can say. I truly believe my life wouldn't be nearly as rich without you in it. Though we're family, I treasure the soul-sister bond we share even more. Thank you for the thoughtful, gentle questions that have helped me reflect and, often, find clarity. Your quiet wisdom has guided me more times than you know. Thanks, too, for all the shopping trips, lunches, phone calls, and texts, which helped me process the rough seasons. I believe God placed you in my life with purpose, and I'm deeply grateful He did.

Amy, for always being there when I needed an ear to listen. I felt so loved, and you taught me how to be a true friend. Your support in our many designing escapades and all the stories shared while hanging out in your sewing room have always lifted me up, helping me get through some difficult times, and will never be forgotten. You were the first person in my life to tell me to "slow down" because "you never know what you will miss when you rush." Our moments together will forever be a treasure in my heart. Lastly, thank you for reviewing my book. It would not have been complete without your part in it!

Kevin Yanskey, for being my "first baby" because I can still remember toting you around when I was about six and you were just nine months old. Thank you for always being there when I needed you for computer issues. Once I was slightly frantic when I thought I lost the whole book file, and you walked me through the steps to retrieve it. You call me when I least expect it, just to talk, and it's so sweet. In addition, when I struggled with self publishing you offered your program manager skills to give me that push I needed to move forward. I am so grateful for you. You were always there and still are!

Don Yanskey for playing farm in the sandbox with me and taking me around with your friends when I was 15 even though you did not have to. I miss those days laughing to all the stand-up comedy 8-track tapes and always enjoyed the years you played the keyboard at church and the bass guitar in your band, Second Wind. I was so happy watching you share your talents. You always make me laugh, and I am forever grateful to you for that.

My Mom, for loving my dad, teaching me discipline and hard work, showing me how to have a "finish the job" attitude and how we could do things better or faster. Thank you for loving me and allowing me to write what I did in my memoir. "If it is what is true for you, then keep it," you said. Thank you for being there for me (even if it's to take beer out of my car before the cops came after I hydroplaned and rear ended the vehicle in front of me at 19). Who can forget all the beautifully sewn quilts you constructed. I know God saw every stitch you made and loves them. Love you, Mom!

My Dad (who passed on March 31, 2014), for working hard on the farm for your family, eating homemade ice cream in the backyard late at night after the farm work was done for the day while listening to the Cardinal game on the radio, working through your own trials with mom by your side, your sense of humor, sharing your "never to forget" one-liners, not knowing a stranger, and for loving my mom. I miss you so much!

Dr. Marvin Shipman, for being a steadfast doctor and friend for over 30 years. Your support has carried us through so much, not just in times of physical illness but through emotional and spiritual battles as well. Your naturopathic wisdom has helped us heal, but it's your unwavering faith and ability to draw us closer to Jesus, the Holy Spirit, and God Almighty that has left the deepest impact. I've always been in awe of how clearly you discern what is not of God and how boldly you help us break free from it. Thank you for taking our calls during the darkest moments, for celebrating our victories, and for offering guidance when we needed clarity. *Will You Do It?* was a question you once asked God quietly and humbly during your own healing journey. He answered with your healing, and your testimony stirred something deep in me. I realized I had been asking the same question all these years in my own way as Julia's mom. Julia and I love you and your beautiful wife, Rebbecca, more than words can say. Thank you, Rebbecca, for supporting Marvin as he so graciously supported us.

Apostle Harvey (from Antioch Fellowship Church, now named Kingdom Life), for being one of my biggest supporters. I shared with you that I was writing a book, and it seemed every time I had writer's block and had laid it aside for a brief time, you would inquire about it. This sparked ideas and memories, which spurred me to open my laptop to write again. I will be forever grateful for your genuine friendship and brotherly love. Your words and encouragement alone were sowing the seed in me to grow my faith and see my book to fruition. You once said, "Don't let anyone stop you!" You are a blessing to me and a true servant of God!

James Snapp (Ed's son), for joyfully allowing your beautiful epilogue to be included in my memoir. It was a generous gift of words that perfectly honored your father. Your contribution means more to me than you know. Thanks for the fond memories you shared. They added depth, warmth and a true sense of who Ed was: a man with hope of all hope.

Heidi Kerby, for meeting me for ice cream cyclones in Lincoln and helping me with travel plans, but mostly for your friendship and consenting to be one of my alpha readers (even though you wondered what you would say to me if you didn't like it!). You are a dear friend. Thank you!

My two Goddaughters, Mackenzie and Brooke, for allowing me to love you and listening to my little nuggets of life lessons. I was so honored to be asked to be your Godmother. I take this position to heart, and I hope I've supported you in your life and helped you in your journey with God, Jesus Christ, and the Holy Spirit.

Ann Marie, for keeping all your old Hallmark calendars you dug through to help me with the timing of your part in our story. What a treasure. Over the years, you became one of Julia's and my dear friend, someone who truly showed up in Julia's life. Thank you. You will never be forgotten! We love you.

Denise Mitchell, for always checking in with us to see how we are doing and being a true lifelong friend. I always enjoy visiting, especially about home designs. It never seems like we have enough time and I always look forward to more. Thank you.

Debbie Hamler, for always stepping up, calling past teachers and friends of the Special Learning Center to join Julia and me for lunch, sharing memories, and helping fill in some missing pieces for my memoir. Your love for every child who has come through those doors over the past 40 years still shines, even in retirement. Volunteering wasn't just something you did, it is who you are. God gave you a servant's heart, and we are so deeply blessed that you chose to share it with us.

Karlee Renkoski (my sweet and professional editor), for being patient, kind, and persevering with me through this writing process with unwavering support. You are another example of how God had his hand in this project. Working with you has been a wonderful experience. Without your journalism background, editing skills, and creative writing, this book would have never gotten finished as smoothly or quickly as it did. You are a true blessing! Working with you was a gift and I am deeply grateful. Thank you.

My little voice, the Holy Spirit. Over the past 30 years, every time I moved the boxes of journals to my next home, I wondered if I should keep them or not. And every time, there was a little voice that told me to "keep them" even though I knew I wasn't a writer. Thank God I listened. It still amazes me that this memoir miracle came true.

About the Author

Marilyn Kay has called mid-Missouri home her entire life and where she raised her children. As a devoted mother, her greatest joy is spending time with her daughters.

Marilyn lives out her calling as a licensed massage therapist, sharing her deep empathy and intuitive touch with every client she serves. Outside of her profession, Marilyn finds joy in singing in her church's praise and worship team, spending time in her garden, and travel.

Lord, Will You Do It? is Marilyn's debut as an author—a piece that began more than twenty years ago. Writing this memoir deepened her faith and drew her closer to God, a journey she continues to cherish.

REFERENCES

http://www.snapptherapy.com/ccdtherapy/understandingccdt.html

Shipman's Healthy and Whole:

https://www.facebook.com/shipmanshealthyandwhole/

Centre for Inner Change, Denver, Colorado, is no longer in business; however, the method is still available:

https://www.tomatis.com/en/the-tomatis-method/

https://cranialsacraltherapy.org/blog/what-is-cranial-sacral-therapy-and-how-can-it-help-you

https://myofascialrelease.com/

https://www.neu.fit/

Frequency Specific Microcurrent:

https://frequencyspecific.com/about/

Leslie Churchill at:

https://www.midcitychiro.com/

There are many more frequency devices and light devices on the market currently that we have never experienced, but I'm praying for God's frequency to heal you or your loved one. Amen!